CHOSEN

ANSWERING THE CALL OF JESUS

ALAN JOHNSTON

SONCOAST PUBLISHING

Chosen

ISBN 979-8-88758-004-3 Paperback

ISBN 979-8-88758-005-0 Ebook

Published by Soncoast Publishing

P.O. Box 1503

Hartselle, AL 35640

www.soncoastpublishing.com

CONTENTS

CHOSEN: ANSWERING THE CALL OF JESUS

"Show me your paths and teach me to follow" Ps. 25:4 CEV

*This book is dedicated to all those men and women
who have heard God's call to service, who have made, and continue to make a
Kingdom sized impact for the gospel.*

*And especially to four of my dearest "preacher buddies,"
all of whom have truly answered the call to follow Jesus.*

*Rev. Herman Parker
Dr. Ron Phillips
Rev. Evie Megginson
Dr. Herb Thomas*

THOSE AMAZING APOSTLES

The Sea of Galilee is a beautiful place, with its picturesque views and its calming atmosphere. There is little wonder that Jesus Christ spent so much time on and around its waters. One day as Jesus strolled along the shores of Galilee, He stopped to talk to a group of fishermen. As they talked, Jesus said to them, *"Come follow me and I will make you a fisher of men."* Jesus repeated that statement, or similar statements, several times. In fact, he did not stop until twelve men heard his challenge to follow him; that is, to become his disciples. Those twelve individuals became the core group of disciples who went on to follow Jesus for three years. In the course of time they witnessed miracles, heard sermons, watched masses come to see and hear him, and saw a ministry develop that would span the centuries. They often struggled to grasp the meaning of what he said or did, but they continued to follow and to learn. That group of twelve became the earliest followers of Jesus and would eventually become known as the apostles. As different as they were, Jesus saw something in each one of them that could be shaped into a communicator of good news (the gospel). For most, the world at that time was a rather bleak place, and for many the idea of hope and joy was not even imagined, and at the very least a faint and fleeting idea. Jesus came to change that, and these twelve individuals would be called and trained to cast their nets to draw the hurting and hopeless to Jesus' message of hope, healing, and heaven.

JESUS CALLING

How does one assemble a team, a staff, an organization? Universities build their athletic teams by recruiting players, runners, rowers, sprinters, gymnasts…whatever the particular sport calls those participants. Professional sports "draft" their participants. Businesses often hire professional "head-hunters" (recruiters) to identify talent that could be pertinent to their business. Jesus faced the daunting task of finding the kind of talent that had the potential to change the course of history, and truly turn the world upside down. His method of selection is described in Luke's gospel, "*In these days he went out to the mountain to pray, and all night he continued in prayer to God. And when day came, he called his disciples and chose them twelve, whom he named apostles….*" Jesus had many learners and followers gathered around him, after all, that is what discipleship means…. following and learning. From that significant sized group, He would need a core of leaders. Leaders who could continue the mission, and maintain the drive and enthusiasm, of all the disciples who answered the call of Jesus. Leaders who would stay the course, even when the boss was not around.

It is not uncommon in today's business climate for certain companies, in searching for a new CEO, to look for a leader who has been branded by business publications as a "turnaround specialist." What is meant by that label is that the leader is going to face many challenges, from within and from without, in the attempt to build a team of people into a highly capable and productive organization. Let's face it, that was the challenge facing Jesus when, at the age of thirty, he faced the challenge of putting together a team of men and women who could become a cohesive unit of fearless followers, who themselves had the potential to become leaders. This book will focus on those followers, and their personal journey to become servant leaders, whose mark on the world would outlive the ages. There was of course at least one exception, but for the most part, Jesus remarkable success, first with the twelve, and then with hundreds of other disciples, changed the world for all eternity.

Were we to try to package Jesus' leadership style, what might we say about it? In today's leadership training systems, there is an almost endless list of opinions about what a good leader does and does not do, as well as labels for the many so-called styles of leadership. One such label is "servant-leader." I was a leadership trainer for the American Express company for many years, and we always talked about the role of a servant in becoming a good leader. Yet, it is not in a textbook or in a classroom that we discover a definition of servant-leader. It is to the Bible we look, and there we see that leadership style modeled in all that Jesus did, both in selecting and training those who were to become his replacement leaders. It has been said many times, great leaders are always training their replacement. Jesus knew he had only three years to get these trainees ready. Goodness, there were many times he simply had to get alone (to pray – which is an excellent idea for any leader) and sort things out. An abundance of questions remained for Jesus the CEO, the who, the what, the where and the when would need to be answered. That's what leaders do.

The heart and mind of Jesus was fixated on service. The Bible records of him, *"For the Son of man did not come to be served, but to serve…."* Far too many of us associate leadership with a seat at the head table. In Luke 14:8-10, Jesus gave us an important lesson regarding the jostling that goes on for seats at the front of the room. In that text Jesus wraps up the lesson with this, *"For everyone who exalts himself will be humbled, and he who humbles himself will be exalted."* Christ-like leadership does not tell or lord over others, rather it works alongside, doing, coaching, encouraging, commending, and yes correcting, as needed. Within the confines of the church I, and others, have come to call this a "towel and basin" mentality. Real leadership is out in the crowd, not seated at the head table. In John's gospel, Jesus demonstrated the towel and basin model when he wrapped a towel around his waist, took a basin of water, and went around the room washing the feet of his disciples.

One of my favorite "old timey" preachers and writers was Leonard Ravenhill. He told a story about a group of tourists who were visiting a lovely village. As they walked past an old man sitting by a fence, one tourist asked him in a patronizing way, "Were any great men born in this village?" The old man replied, "Nope, only babies." That is a great segue to my belief that leadership is developed, not discovered. Yes, it is true that certain "born leaders" tend to emerge, but to stay on their game those natural leadership qualities need to be developed.

MEET THE MEN

There is something to be learned from the lives of these twelve and their relationships with Jesus. As we retrace their steps, watch their actions, and listen to their words we quickly discover that as amazing as these apostles were, they remained very human. There were plenty of mistakes. Some, like Peter, often misspoke, and then there was the time James and John (encouraged by their mother) asked Jesus for prominent positions in his coming Kingdom. A few of them were political radicals. For all his followers, their collective weaknesses were chided by Jesus as he sought to correct and corral their passions. Their stories are cluttered with disillusionment, denials, doubts and even death. In those early years of their travels with Jesus they were anything but a finished product, but remember, Jesus chose them not because of who or what they were, but they were chosen because of who they could become. These individuals were not merely traveling companions and close friends of Jesus. They were more than mere associates. After learning from the master teacher and allowing God to gain full control of their personality and temperaments, they would take the message of hope to the masses and it would eventually be said of them, "These...*have turned the world upside down...*" (Acts 17:6). They shattered the face of the ancient world and changed the course of history. They faced a daunting task – take the message of Jesus Christ into a world filled

4

with hate and hostility – and in doing so – expecting it to change the world.

Never forget that these were not individuals who had attended elite schools and earned degrees that would have prepared them for their assignment. In fact, in Acts, Luke refers to them as *"unlearned and ignorant men."* They possessed no real wealth or social status. They were primarily ordinary citizens living in a country that was controlled by a foreign military power. How could they dare dream of evangelizing the world? "Mission Impossible" would seem an appropriate title for a book detailing their exploits. Yet, these men, through the transforming presence and message of Jesus Christ, would explode on the scene as a dynamic force operating under a divine imperative.

SHAPED AND SHARPENED FOR SERVICE

Everything we do – family, church, career, school, financial and other important decisions, relationships (including God), habits – and so much more, are all what they are because of our temperaments (personality). Just look at the twelve apostles, what a diverse collection of individuals. Glance around the church sanctuary – what a collection! How about some of those weird folks at work, how did they get to be so (fill in the blank). Rock and Roll singer Jerry Lee Lewis had a hit song titled, *"You've Got Personality."* As he croons along, he describes why he is madly in love, apparently, even at times acting foolish. He describes some of the admirable attributes of the one on whom he has set his affections – walk, talk, a smile, and charm – well, you get the idea. Interspersed with those attributes he interjects, *"You've got personality…."* That person whom he admired was endowed with attributes that oozed personality. As you see, we all have personality, and it is who we are.

Jesus, with his mission in mind, did what good leaders do. He pulled together a team. That team was comprised of varied talent, experiences, and personality. He set about teaching them what they would need to know and do in order to replace him once he was gone. Once trained, he could then entrust the job to them, and having trained them, have the expectation that he could then hold them accountable for completing the job. Tandem to that he would have to provide management for their development. Jesus no doubt considered their personalities by tailoring their training agenda so that it would align with their personality (temperament).

Lest you think I have gone off track here, let's be reminded that every family, every church, every business, and every organization is impacted by the personality of every person in that group. Most groups will have an uninhibited and even egotistical member like Peter. It is likely that the group will have one who is capable of hostility and who can at times have an unreasonable mindset. The apostle Paul certainly fits into that category. Others in your group may be like the apostle John, who was highly sensitive, studious and at the same time could tilt toward the hostile side. The studious Matthew became the fund raiser and business manager for the disciples (CFO). Judas was the accountant and treasurer. Andrew appears to have been the chairman of the board and authorized spending for the group. Philip was named quartermaster, which meant keeping the traveling band of disciples fed and supplied. His job also included finding food for the crowds that followed Jesus. No doubt, Jesus found something in their personalities that equipped them for their assignments.

There are many tools and so-called "testing instruments" that can be used to assess personality. The tool that I found easiest to learn, remember and apply is called the Social Styles Model. Its premise is that every person will have a preferred way of acting, thinking and making decisions (social style). The four social styles are called Driver, Expressive, Amiable, and Analytic. Each style has its own way of using time, interacting, and making decisions. Individuals will have a dominant style which is typically blended with a secondary style. Research indicates that a person under pressure will always revert to their dominant style. This tool readily enables one to observe a person and determine their preference or style. One can then adapt behaviors to make the other person more comfortable, and therefore, increase the likelihood of successful interactions.

The numerous assessment tools have merit and could be useful in assessing personality style. Jesus needed no such tools for he could read the hearts and minds of those early followers. Scripture tells us that Jesus knew from the beginning that Judas would eventually betray him, thus he equally knew the hearts of the other eleven.

All of us have a blended personality relative to style and type. Our temperament, as personality is sometimes called, is a blend of our parental genetics combined with certain learned behaviors.

Jesus placed people in roles and positions that gave them the greatest opportunity for success and personal fulfillment. He matched personality to assignments. However, the most important component of the success of those who followed Jesus had a direct correlation to how much control of their life they willingly surrendered to Jesus.

SPIRIT CONTROLLED TEMPERAMENT

Tim LaHaye published a book (1967) titled "Spirit Controlled Temperaments." LaHaye was a Bible teacher and faith-based counselor. He contended that our temperament is who we really are. It is about genetics, it is about life experiences, it is about the influences that have come to bear on our life. It speaks to character. In a second book which LaHaye titled, "Transformed Temperaments," he goes to great lengths in reminding us that the Holy Spirit has transforming power that not only applies to our salvation, but also shaping us into who and what God wants us to be. Frankly, this takes away some of our excuses for poor behavior – behavior that is not comely for a Christian. If our temperamental propensities sometimes get us in trouble or embarrass us, perhaps it is because we have failed to subject them to the Holy Spirit. Surely, we recognize that a cursing Simon Peter or a doubting Thomas were not under the influence of the Holy Spirit in those precise moments. The cure for these unbecoming moments is surrendering to and being filled with the Holy Spirit. The Bible says, "*Be continually filled with the Spirit.*" (Ephesians 5:18) The Bible also says in Galatians 5:16 "*...walk in the Spirit, and you will not gratify the desires of* *the flesh against the Spirit.*" Total transformation comes through one's personal relationship with Jesus Christ and is continually available through the facilitation of the Holy Spirit. What does it mean to be filled with the Holy Spirit? It certainly must contain an element of confession, for the Bible says, "*If I cherish iniquity in my heart, the Lord will not have listened*" (Psalm 66:18). The good news relative to being cleansed of sin is recorded in 1 John 1:9, "*If we confess our sins, he is faithful and just to forgive us our sins and to cleanse us of all unrighteousness.*" The filling of the Holy Spirit is aptly defined in a term that I have heard successful coaches from all sorts of athletic team's state that the team won a game or match because the players all "left everything on the field/court today." Obviously, the coach meant that they held nothing back. They gave their all. In other words, they were totally committed. The same commitment is required of Christians who want to live continuously filled with the Holy Spirit. The apostle Paul said, "*I appeal to you therefore, brothers, by the mercies of God, to present your bodies as a living sacrifice, holy and acceptable to God…*" (Romans 12:1). Clearly, God wants all that we are – mind, body, and spirit – committed to him. Be assured that such a level of commitment will lead to conflict. For Christians, we live in a world that is not our home. That world currently "groans," according to Romans 8:22-23, under the weight of the fallen nature of mankind. The day-to-day actions of this world are controlled by "*…the schemes of the devil. We…wrestle…against the rulers, against authorities, against cosmic powers over this present darkness, against the spiritual forces of evil in heavenly places.*" (Ephesians 6:12) We are foolish to think or believe that we are any match for such an enemy. Only by being filled with and walking in the Holy Spirit will we prevail. Paul says, "*…we are not waging war according to the flesh. For the weapons of our warfare are not of the flesh but have divine power to destroy.*" (2 Corinthians 10:3-4) In Christ the victory is ours!

One of the verses in the great old Martin Luther hymn, "A Mighty Fortress is our God," says it so well.

And tho this world with devils be filled,
Should threaten to undo us,

8

We will not fear, for God hath willed
His truth to triumph thru us.
The prince of darkness grim
We tremble not for him – his rage we can endure,
For lo, his ruin is sure:
One little word shall fell him.

So yes, may every Christian prepare for battle, be filled with the Spirit and, "*Therefore take up the whole armor of God, that you may be able to stand in the evil day, and having done all, to stand firm*" (Ephesians 6:13). Spirit filled and Spirit controlled lives equips us for anything and everything.

ORDINARY TO EXTRAORDINARY

The Revelation calls the twelve apostles the foundation stones of the Christian church. There are four lists that contain the names the apostles in the Bible: Matthew 10:2-4; Mark 3:16-19; Luke 6:14-16; Acts 1:13. As you examine the lists you will find that Peter is listed first in each list. It is also noteworthy that Judas Iscariot is not included in the list found in Acts. With the exclusion of Judas from the list, we momentarily meet the hastily chosen Matthias, but then he all but disappears. It then becomes crystal clear that Paul (Saul of Tarsus) will become the replacement for Judas Iscariot.

By tracing the life of these individuals, it is seen that they experienced and enjoyed many hours of victory. But there were also times of doubt, worry, fear, stress, uncertainly, and even a moment or two of unbelief. They were quite ordinary, yet their encounter with Jesus Christ made them extraordinary. They did not become an instant success in ministry, even though they had spent countless hours, days, and months with Jesus. Clearly, their first step toward being extraordinary was their nothing-held-back surrender of everything to Jesus. There would not be any success without total submission. Only when they became "*doers of the Word*" (James 1:22), were they positioning themselves for the extraordinary. While Jesus was immediately available to them they operated through his anointing and power. He told them that after he was gone there would be another who would come alongside them (the Holy Spirit) and that he would provide presence, anointing and power. Here is the exciting part – any Christian, wholly surrendered to Jesus, and walking in the presence of God, having Holy Spirit anointing and experiencing the power of God – is positioned for the extraordinary.

The next time you sit in a church sanctuary, take a minute, glance around at the faces of the people sitting around you. Other than not having seen Jesus, they are no different than the individuals that appear in this book. Common people, from common places, mostly doing common work – until they allowed Jesus to become to the most important person or thing in their lives. Jesus is still looking for the common who are willing to do the uncommon things for the Kingdom of God. In 1 Corinthians 1: 26-29, Paul said, *"For consider your calling, brothers, not many of you were wise according to the worldly standards, not many were powerful, not many of noble birth. But God chose what is foolish in the world to shame the wise; God chose what is weak in the world to shame the strong; God chose what is low in the world, even the things that are not, to bring to nothing the things that are; so that no human being might boast in the presence of God…."*

Who is the next Andrew? The next Simon Peter? The next John? They are among us today. Jesus' invitation of *"Come follow me"* did not end with the last apostle, or the last great disciple in the Bible. Jesus continues to call, and frankly, fully expects us to affirm that call with fully yielded minds and hearts.

The apostles, who were remarkably diverse in so many ways, were united in a common purpose by an uncommon person. Jesus took the expressive/driver temperament of Simon Peter and created in him a leader and a bold preacher. In Matthew's amiable/expressive style Jesus found one who, once removed from a detested profession and fully transformed, would become an honorable and trusted disciple. In the government hating and hot – headed Simon the Zealot Jesus saw a passion, if redirected, that could produce Kingdom sized results. The sometimes negative, analytical, naysayer of the bunch, Thomas, found a place alongside

Jesus that would not end until his own death in India. In the same way that Jesus Christ called and changed all these early followers He is still changing and calling us to "come follow me." It is my hope and prayer that all those who read this book will fully understand that all of us, not just a select few, not just those who ooze talent and personality, not just those who practice their spiritual gifts with a title (pastor, evangelist, teacher, apostle), but all of us have a calling to service in the Kingdom of God.

As a Freshman at Samford University, sitting in an Old Testament class taught by Dr. Sigurd Bryan, I became enthralled with the story of Isaiah the Prophet's call and his response to that call. It contains a valuable lesson for all of us. In Isaiah chapter six the prophet has had a "mind-blowing" visitation from God that included a vision with multiple lessons. These words are found in Isaiah 6:8, *"And I heard the voice of the Lord saying, 'whom shall I send, and who will go for us?' Then I said, here am I, send me."* Dr. Bryan pointed out that "whom" is plural and "who" is singular. The obvious implication is that God wants all His people to answer the call to Christian service, yet it is the "few" who upon hearing, respond with "Send me." May this book prompt more of us to consider God's claim and call on our life, and in so doing align ourselves with the "few" who live their life fully surrendered and committed to Jesus.

Now let's meet these disciples who said yes to the invitation to follow Jesus. Among those disciples, some who were later called the apostles, we find men and women, young and older, who all came to not only know Christ, but also answered the call to *"Come follow me."*

2

PETER: THE APOSTLE OF FIRE

R ocky stumbled and staggered around the ring, struggling to remain upright as punch after punch added to his pain and misery. Bruised and bleeding, the overmatched part-time fighter and part-time bill collector took blow after blow, but after a thirteen round fight he was still standing. That 1976 movie, "Rocky," spawned eight sequels. Today most can readily remember the legacy created by Rocky's reputation as a fighter. Long before the movie, the Bible introduces us to another fighter named the Rock. We, of course, also know the Rock as Simon Peter.

Peter is named first in all the lists of the twelve disciples given in the New Testament. Peter is the most common name of the man who became known as a rock. He is called by three other names in the Bible. He was called Simon in the most intimate parts of his relationship with Jesus. He was also called Simon as we observe him in his domestic life, such as "Simon's house" or "Simon's wife's mother." He is also called Simeon since that is the original Hebrew form of his name. Then of course he is also called Cephas, because Cephas is the Aramaic form of the word rock.

Of the apostles, none have as much material written about them as does Peter. The Gospels are full of Peter. It has been suggested that the reason for this bulk of material is due to the close relationship between Mark and Peter. Peter thought of Mark as his son, and more than a few have suggested that Mark's gospel is actually the preaching material of Peter. Peter concealed nothing, telling of his own mistakes, recounting all the rebukes and frequent lectures from Jesus.

No apostle speaks as often as Peter, nor does Jesus speak as often to anyone as he does Peter. There are times when he is praised, and at other times he was on the receiving end of corrective discipline. Peter was reproved by Jesus more than any other disciple. No other would dare to reprove Jesus, yet Peter attempted to do so. Every group must have a leader and Peter was seemingly the natural leader of this group. Based on his personality type, he was likely accustomed to talking or pushing his way to the front of any group or any issue. His personality would have driven him deepest into a cave, to swim farthest in the sea, or to climb higher up the mountain than any other. That was simply his competitive nature.

He is seen as the first to speak, first to act. He could be impulsive and impetuous, tempestuous and talented, enthusiastic, extreme, and extroverted; Jesus saw in him the potential to be Rocky.

CHARACTERISTICS OF THE MAN

Peter was from the city of Bethsaida, a small town on the shores of Galilee, from which Jesus often worked and taught. For Peter to be transformed into Rocky was not an easy path. Our Rocky, like the Rocky in the movie, was going to need a trainer. The movie version of Rocky had Mickey for a trainer. Our Rocky had Jesus for a trainer.

Peter was never at a loss for words to say; in fact, he never learned that sometimes "silence is golden." I too, on many occasions, have to be reminded that sometimes silence is the best course of action. Silence is not a character trait that comes naturally for me, and like Peter, I have often spoken when I should have been silent. He was the type of person who always enjoyed the company of others, and it is rare to find him alone. He found himself in many difficult situations of his own making. Now, given his fiery personality, Peter was likely ready to fight his way, verbally and physically, out of those situations. He seldom lacked enthusiasm in any of his pursuits. His disposition, as some would say, allowed his mouth to overload his ability to walk away from trouble. He may not have always been correct, but he always had an opinion, and everyone was going to hear that opinion.

While Peter could be prone to violence, he could also prove himself virtuous. Though on a few occasions his behavior was cowardly, he could also be courageous. There were times, such as the evening when Jesus was arrested, that Peter was overcome with fear, but he soon replaced that fear with staunch fidelity. Of the twelve, he was only one who dared to walk on water, yet he sank because of a sudden attack of fear. He was the only one who challenged the soldier, yet he fled at the voice of a maiden. He dared to challenge the Lord, yet he was always ready to admit his mistakes. He was easily drawn into sin, but just as readily he confessed his sin. Even though many weaknesses existed in Peter's character, Jesus saw him as Rocky, the fighter, the guy who would get up off the mat when struck down, the guy would never give up. It ought to be of great comfort to every saint of every age that Jesus looks beyond who we are to who we can become. Peter became a rock by spending time with Jesus. The Lord is yet ready to take people as they are and transform them into something beautiful and useful.

I can think of several terms that give us a hint regarding the characteristics of Peter. The first word is humility. This is the characteristic that made the difference in Peter and Judas. Both denied Jesus, but it was the humility of Peter which saved him from the kind of despair that led Judas to suicide. The trait of humility was clearly on display in the incident that led to Peter being rebuked by Paul (Acts 15). In that incident Peter didn't defend or rationalize his behavior, but took it as an opportunity to learn and grow. Humility is at the foundation of any relationship, and certainly our relationship with Christ.

A second word which is applicable to the life of Peter is failure.

Peter knew what it was to fail. Many times, he was rash and impulsive and spoke without thinking. This fact about Peter resulted in many mishaps in his life. In one instance as the disciples were out on the sea, a storm arose and they were afraid. As the intensity of the storm grew, Jesus suddenly appeared and was coming to them, walking on the water. Peter blindly went over the side of the boat and walked toward Jesus. Then suddenly realizing what he was doing, fear overcame him, and he sank.

In another scene Peter confesses that Jesus is the Christ, the Son of God. Jesus explained that this confession was not from Peter but from God. It was then that Jesus said Peter would become a rock. But no sooner said, the rock begins to show stress cracks. Jesus began to tell of his persecution and death, and Peter said to Jesus that this could never happen to him. Jesus rebuked him, *"Get behind me Satan! You are a hindrance to me."* Peter had failed again.

Once again, this time in the upper room, Peter speaks when he should have kept quiet. Jesus explains that every one of the disciples will forsake him. True to his character, Peter blurts out that he will not forsake Jesus. Yet, just a few hours later, Peter is standing by a campfire in Jerusalem, denying having ever known Jesus. Then looking into the face of Jesus, Peter ran off and wept bitterly. Peter knew that he could not possibly be a bigger failure than at that moment.

Our Christian experience is littered with struggles. There are the times of doubt and despair that result in a spiritual disconnect in our relationship with Jesus. Each of us can reflect on times of denial that match the behavior of Peter in that garden. I have had experiences, as did Simon Peter, when because of my own actions, I have felt as though I was drowning in a sea of unbelief, and even unrepentance. Like Peter, I have often been my own worst enemy. Actions, attitudes, unbiblical alliances… on and on goes the list. Whether it be a denial by some overt act, or a denial buried and hidden in our heart, it matters not. Failure is failure is failure.

The important thing is that Peter overcame his failures, and with each act of repentance and recovery moved a step closer to becoming the Rocky Jesus knew he could be. What sad commentary is being strung together by so many believers who, rather than moving from victory to victory, continue a downward path strewn with failure. There is no victory, there is not a time of renewal. While there is certain to be failure, there must also be a time of getting up from the defeat, and in Jesus finding the courage to fight again. Scripture does not hide the truth; rather, it reminds us that we are in battle every day. We have choices. Some elect to quit. Others choose to stay down on the mat and commiserate. Still others will get up and fight again, without changing their strategy, only to be knocked down again. Others, turning to the wisdom of their trainer, Jesus, will become overcomers. Peter learned how to be an overcomer. With each knockdown he turned to Jesus and found the faith, energy and strategy to get up a winner.

A third characteristic of Peter is found in the word, outspoken. That describes Peter, for better or worse. There were many times his quick tongue got him in trouble, and Jesus once remarked that Peter had allowed himself to be the spokesman for Satan. However, Pentecost brought a remarkable change in Peter. He did not grow quiet or reserved, but He allowed the filling of the Holy Spirit to control his thoughts, actions and words. This aspect of Peter's transformational experience became a turning point in the life of the early church.

Peter was always frank, speaking his mind regardless of the circumstances. He evolved into the spokesperson for the other apostles. He would ask the questions that others hesitated to ask. He was always willing to state the opinion of the others, make suggestions, speak when they did not have the courage to speak.

Every Christian ought to pray that the Lord would keep them from "putting their foot in their mouth," but we should also pray for boldness and courage to speak truth and to speak when directed by the Lord. Our words matter! Life and death are in our hands…that is, our ability and willingness to tell the gospel story. Yes, heaven and hell are in the balances, and the outcome for someone may well depend on us.

CALLED BY THE MASTER

Simon Peter was introduced to the Lord in an indirect manner. Peter was introduced to Jesus by his brother Andrew. Andrew and John had been with John the Baptist in the wilderness when the Baptist proclaimed, *"Behold the Lamb of God."* John and Andrew followed Jesus and soon found themselves spending the day with Jesus. Following that conversation, Andrew went and found his brother Peter, and told him about the One he had found.

No doubt, Peter had also been a disciple of John the Baptist, and he, like the others, longed for the coming of the Messiah. Andrew had heard the message of the Baptist, and his personal encounter with Jesus led him to quickly return to find Peter and share with him his life-changing discovery.

After this initial contact with Jesus, there came a distinct time of decision in Peter's life. After having met Jesus, Peter returned to Capernaum and took up in his vocation of fishing. He, along with Andrew, James, and John were, as we know, successful fishermen. Their business was located in Galilee, in and around Capernaum.

Like everyone, Peter arrived at a point where he had to make a definitive decision about Jesus. You see, there is no middle ground with Jesus. Jesus once said, *"You are either for me or against me."* Tragically, the Bible is filled with those who chose against Jesus. Their lot is lost forever. Triumphantly, the Bible is also filled with those who chose Jesus. We revel in those glorious decisions. Of the many conversions in the Bible, I marvel most at the story of the Samaritan women who met Jesus at Jacob's well. She went for a drink of water but left with an inner river of water that would never run dry. Her story doesn't stop there. By the time we read the end of the story (John 4), that woman, who remains nameless – but whose name is forever written in heaven, led an entire town to meet Christ. That's how the gospel is meant to work. Finding Christ for ourselves…then telling another, who tells another, who tells another. For Peter that time of decision came while he was on the job. Perhaps Peter often reminisced of that first meeting with Jesus. Jesus had immediately recognized him as Simon Barjona (son of John).

But the strange thing to Peter was that Jesus had said he would be called Cephas, or rock.

Without reservation Jesus had quickly seen qualities in Peter that He could rely on to build His church. Though Peter did not comprehend what Jesus meant, it would be just a matter of some three years before he would fully grasp what was Jesus had meant, and what He expected Peter to do in the Kingdom.

Peter, raised in Jewish traditions, as were other Jewish boys, would have attended a synagogue school. There he was taught the Scriptures, especially from the Law and the Prophets. From the synagogue Peter knew that a Messiah had been promised to Israel. Though the testimony of Luke in Acts indicates Peter did not receive any special rabbinical training, Peter was still aware of the great hope of Israel. Soon he would be invited to forsake the fishing nets and begin casting a net for the souls of others.

The challenge and the call to follow Jesus came one morning as Peter returned from a night of fishing. The business partners had been out on the water all night. They had cast their nets through the night to no avail, their efforts had proved futile. Such experienced fishermen seldom failed to such an extent. They were eager to go home, wash their nets in preparation for the next fishing trip, then eat and crash into their beds. Their plans were about to make an "about face."

Suddenly Jesus, pushed along by a large crowd, got into the boat and requested that they launch out into the lake. As they got over deep water Jesus made what seemed to Peter a foolish request. Jesus said, *"Let down your nets for a great catch."* Peter was an expert in his trade, and he knew this was the wrong time to fish because the rising sun had already created a bright glare on the water. If he were to lower his net while the sun was bright, he would be the laughingstock of those on the shore. However, Peter did as he was told. The result became the turning point for Peter in his realization that Jesus was no ordinary man. Peter became conscious that there was a presence of a power within this Galilean preacher, a power that Peter had never experienced, a power that demanded attention.

In the invitation from Jesus Christ to Peter it is readily seen that the Lord was not merely calling men to be his followers, Jesus was calling Peter and the others so that they might be trained (discipled), and in turn disciple others. The call of Christ to men and women today is much the same. He calls us not only to salvation but also to become involved in the redemptive process of telling the world about salvation. Jesus does not call people to live in isolation. We, like Peter and those other disciples, are saved, and then sent to make disciples of others. Then and now, the responsibility remains the same.

Peter became a disciple, a learner and follower, a student in training for ministry. Jesus, of course, had many disciples, hundreds, if not thousands. Peter, like so many others, sought to follow Jesus and glean all they could from Him. Peter was also an apostle. An apostle is one who was sent out to be an official representative of Jesus. Somewhat along the line of what Paul would later refer to as *"ambassadors for Christ."* Paul said that God had entrusted his message of reconciliation to those ambassadors. The mandate of an ambassador is to represent the wishes of the one who sent him or her. Like an ambassador, an apostle has an official assignment. Today every believer has an assignment, and with that assignment a responsibility to represent the Kingdom that sent us. Christians are stationed in a foreign country (this world) as ambassadors of the Kingdom of God. Like Peter, when we hear the call of Christ and accept the call, we become disciples, trainees, learning all we can from Christ. Then comes the day we are ready to move out, to complete our God-given assignment.

Upon responding to the call of Christ, many changes came about in Peter's life. One of the most obvious changes was in his name. In Matthew 16:18 the name Peter is used rather than Simon. Peter is an Aramaic word from Kepha which means a rock. It is here, tucked away in a corner of Caesarea Philippi, that Simon became Rocky. No, Rocky was far from perfect. Yes, Rocky had a lot to learn. Yet, as the Bible records, Rocky came out punching – after all, Jesus had just told him, along with the others, that hell was no match for them. Jesus is, of course, the "Solid Rock" upon which the church is built. At the same time Peter and all other believers are stones laid upon the foundation, *"...you come to Him...you yourselves like living stones are being built up as a spiritual house..."* (1 Peter 2:4). Peter never forgot nor neglected his calling.

CREATED BY THE MASTER

Let's face it...only Jesus could turn a rough, cussing fisherman into an evangelist. The key words of Jesus as recorded in the Bible are, *"I will make you."* That's right, when it comes to Peter's significant contribution to the Kingdom of God, he was not a "self-made man." It was Jesus Christ living and working within Peter that he was transformed not only into a believer, but also a pillar of faith, devotion and spiritual works, all attributable to the work of Christ in Peter's life. When I consider Peter's selection for such a significant and world-changing role, I cannot help but remember the words of Paul in 1 Corinthians 1:26-31. It serves as a reminder to most of us as we reflect on our own "call" into Kingdom service: *"For consider your calling, brothers; not many of you were wise according to worldly standards, not many were powerful, not many were of noble birth. But chose what is foolish in the world to shame the wise; God chose what is weak in the world to shame the strong; God chose what is low and despised in the world to bring to nothing things that are...."* When Peter and Andrew heard the call of Jesus, they heard the Lord say, *"I will make you fishers of men."* At that point Andrew begins to move into the background, and Simon Peter steps to the front, and before the story ends Peter had become the greatest soul winner of the early church. What Peter became, and what Peter did, was attributable to what the Lord did with him. Even when the material seemed a bit rough and of questionable quality, the Lord was able to shape Peter into someone who was instrumental in changing the lives of thousands of people.

It was not overnight that Simon became Rocky. It was a slow process of teaching, correcting, watching and directing on the part of Jesus. Simon was a hardworking, hot hearted, impetuous Jew who would become leader of the apostolic band.

However, a look at Peter at the time of his calling reveals the fact that Peter had many, many lessons to learn. As with the others, Peter was unlearned, superstitious, and prejudiced. Yet in all of them the Lord saw what no one else could see. In Peter he saw a rock. The rock was surely hidden. It was covered with the moss of a self-life, but it was there.

First, Peter needed to learn the lesson of restraint. Peter had a knack for reacting in an explosive way. When Jesus was arrested in Gethsemane, Peter drew his sword and was ready to fight. There Peter had to learn that our zeal can hinder the cause of Christ. Under the careful, watchful eye of Jesus, Peter was taught to curb his impulsive ways. Self-restraint was to become a part of Peter, but it was unnatural to him; it was a learned characteristic.

An essential lesson for Peter was the lesson of grace. Apparently, Peter found it difficult to forgive his enemies. Once he asked, *"Lord, how often will my brother sin against me, and I forgive him? As many as seven times?"* Peter had to learn a lesson that many of us struggle to grasp…we must learn the lesson that Jesus taught over and over, even in the Model Prayer found in Matthew 6. That lesson is this, in order to be forgiven, we must willingly forgive. Divine forgiveness is much more than just getting rid of resentment or grudges. It represents complete reconciliation. It is a good thing for Peter, and all saints, that the Lord put no limit on grace. If he had limited his grace, none of us would find an open door inviting us into heaven.

Along with so many, Peter struggled with the matter of personal sacrifice. So, we have yet another lesson that needed to be pressed into the heart of Peter. After having answered the call of Jesus, it was soon apparent that this was no easy life they had adopted. In Matthew chapter 16 Christ spoke of the coming rejection, the cross and the grave. Jesus spoke of making great sacrifices, but Peter stepped in with a rebuke. Peter could not understand why this one they called "Lord" would need to make any sacrifices. Well, 'Ole Peter was in for another lesson from the teacher himself. Jesus turned to Peter and rebuked the devil who was controlling the thoughts and words of Peter. Remember, this interaction took place immediately following Jesus having told Peter that he was giving him a new name, Rocky. Basically, Peter, similar to the offer of Satan at the wilderness temptation of Jesus, adhered to the notion that Jesus should be able to serve without any sacrifice. In other words, Peter envisioned a crown without a cross. Jesus fully knew that in God's Kingdom there could be no crown without a cross. May we never forget that our service is genuine only when it is sacrificial. It has been well stated that there can never be an Easter nor Pentecost without Calvary.

Clearly, one of the most difficult lessons for Simon Peter to learn was the concept of a new Kingdom. Jesus came to usher in a new Kingdom, a new society that ran counterculture to popular Jewish beliefs. Like all loyal Jews, Peter's aspirations were for the Messiah to establish a kingdom and set up his rule among Jews. To him salvation was for the Jews.

. In other words, Peter was struggling with the idea that the Kingdom of God had no boundaries. None! God's Kingdom is wide open…any race, any ethnicity, any culture is invited. Entrance into the Kingdom is based on grace alone. Scripture says, *believe on the Lord Jesus Christ and be saved.*" Peter's biased and highly prejudiced view was later corrected as Peter was sent to minister to the household of Cornelius (a Gentile). Peter had to learn that in Christ, Jew and Gentile labels do not exist. I began my own ministry in 1969 in the deep South. One Sunday morning, as was my custom each Sunday, I stood greeting congregants as they made their exit from the sanctuary. I was the pastor of an inner-city church, located in a rapidly changing community. At my behest the deacons, both to my surprise and delight, agreed we would have an open-door policy. As I stood shaking hands that wintery Sunday morning a dear lady, dressed in her mink coat, leaned in as though to whisper, and to this day I remember her exact words, "Brother Alan, do we have to get this kind in here?" She didn't stutter, and I knew what she meant. I replied with the only thing that quickly came to my mind, "Well, my dear, the Bible does say 'Whosoever will, may come.'" I do not pretend to know how God may have dealt with her heart, but I do know from Acts 10 that God dealt with Peter through a vision and visit to the home of Cornelius. Peter learned that God is no respecter of persons. Indeed, whosoever will, may come!

Peter's lessons were not complete…another lesson that Peter had to learn was the lesson of selfless love. The absence of love in our service for the Kingdom leads to ineffectiveness. In 1 Corinthians 13 Paul reminds us that the absence of love in Christian service renders all that is done null and void. Paul congratulated the Corinthians on the presence of all the spiritual gifts in their church, but he also said that the exercise of any of those gifts without love, rendered those efforts nothing more than a lot of loud noise. The absence of love in a marriage turns matrimony into acrimony. The absence of love in a family turns nurture into neglect. The absence of love in a society turns values into violence. The absence of love in a church turns faithfulness into faithlessness, and according to Paul results in a bunch of noisy, but Christless churches. The absence of love in a nation destroys its glory, replacing it with greed and godlessness.

Once Jesus asked, *"Peter…do you love me more than these?"* What did Jesus mean by "these"? Perhaps Jesus meant the fishing business, the boats that he owned, the business that provided income for him and his family, or *"these"* could have easily been a reference to the other disciples. Peter was able to reply, *"Yes Lord, you know that I love you."* Evidence that Peter's reply to Jesus was in fact true is found in Peter's reply to a beggar (Acts 3) asking for a little money. Peter said, *"I have no silver and gold, but what I do have I give you. In the name of Jesus of Nazareth, rise up and walk!"* Peter had become a lover of his Savior, and as well, the souls of the lost, the needy and the hurting.

Following Pentecost, Peter became even more fervent in his passion for the Kingdom, and his love for Christ burned even hotter. In the face of severe opposition, Peter never wilted. Jewish officials were outraged at the work of the disciples, and Peter and John were arrested and brought before the council. The courage of Peter comes to the forefront in those events. Earlier, in a similar situation, Peter had denied the Lord, but not now. He boldly stood for Jesus Christ, stating that he had no choice but tell the story of Jesus. Peter was filled with the Holy Spirit and remained calm and courageous in the face of relentless accusations and threats.

COMMISSIONED BY THE MASTER

Peter's commission from the Lord, put simply, was a commission to witness, win and work. By the way, that same commission is given to every believer. For Peter, his commission included being a missionary and church planter. Within the first twelve chapters of the book of Acts Peter is the most recognizable agent for the new Kingdom. He was the most visible spokesperson for the Christian movement.

Perhaps the commission of Peter extends back to the time when the Lord said, *"I will give you the keys of the Kingdom of heaven...."* The purpose of a key is to turn a lock and open a door. The keys represent the responsibility and privilege of proclaiming the gospel. Opening the door included opening it wide and inviting people to walk through the door. The pattern for opening the door had been given to the disciples and is recorded in Acts chapter one. It would begin with the Jews, spread to the Samaritans, and ultimately include all Gentiles. Once the door has been opened, it never closes.

The Scriptures reveal Peter opening doors for the sheep to enter and then feeding the sheep as Jesus had commanded (John 21) him to do. The early church father, Origen, said, "He who has Peter's faith is the rock of the church, and he who has Peter's virtues keeps the keys to the kingdom." Every child of God has the power of God and the keys of the Kingdom at his or her disposal. Who have you let in lately?

Peter's commission took him to the Jews of the dispersion, that is, those who fled Jerusalem because of religious persecution. It appears that Peter likely spent several years in Syria. This was a region with many Jewish communities, and it seems that the Jews who dispersed into Syria numbered several hundred thousand people. Peter worked as a missionary for some time in that area.

Peter travelled about from church to church and from town to town working among the Jews. Every place he went his influence was validated, and his presence made a lasting impression on those who saw and heard him.

While the New Testament itself is basically silent, Christian tradition connects Peter with three specific ministry locations

He is connected first with Antioch. Some claim him to have been the first bishop of Antioch, and that he served the church for seven years. It was in Antioch that the gospel was first preached to Gentiles and that followers of Christ were called Christians.

It is also believed that Peter traveled into Asia Minor. It is assumed that after leaving Antioch Peter preached in Asia Minor; after all, some of his writing is addressed to the Christians who are scattered throughout Pontus, Galatia, Cappadocia, Asia, and Bithynia.

As would later become true of Paul, a third area to which Peter is connected to is Rome. It is thought that Peter probably went to Rome around 61 A.D. While there is no Biblical evidence of Peter's visit there, legend places him there.

Regardless of where Peter might have been, one thing is certain, he preached Christ. He had been given the highest commission that one can receive, and this version of a transformed Peter always gave of his best to the Master.

COMMITTED TO THE MASTER

The life of Simon Peter is characterized by his bold, courageous and all-out commitment to the Lord. As we read the Bible it seems that no matter where we find Peter there was never any question of his rock sure faith. Prisons held no threat for Peter. Threats never quietened Peter from preaching the gospel. The thought of death never deterred Peter from his passionate commitment to keep telling the story of Jesus again and again, in any venue. We have no clear evidence of how Pete's life ended. Jesus seemed to have indicated, in his conversations with Peter, that death on a cross awaited Peter. The method or the place of his death is not of great importance. The important fact is that Peter never flinched, never gave up, never stopped living out his mandate to take the gospel to the world. Our modern church could certainly use a few more, who like Simon Peter, become an apostle of fire.

3

MATTHEW: THE APOSTLE WHO FOLLOWED

W ow! Some selection, huh? It is very likely that few, if any, of us would have made this selection. As an avid fan of college football I tend to pay close attention to all of various recruiting services which rank the football talent of high school players, and which colleges are in pursuit of certain individuals. Obviously, I am most interested in which players are most likely headed to my alma mater. Some player selections are "head scratchers." One theoretically asks of the coaches, "What were they thinking?" I cannot but help think that many folks, including some of his already chosen disciples, were throwing glances at each other when they learned that Jesus had recruited Levi the tax collector to join their team. Had Jesus not read the scouting reports on this guy? Sure, he made a lot of money, and was able to buy things that ordinary folk could only dream of owning. But nobody liked this guy! He was irksome and the Jewish citizenry were repulsed by the very thought of him. Levi was an outcast, despised by all, yet the day came when Jesus said to him, "Follow me," and follow Jesus he did.

Beyond his original call and his response to the invitation of Jesus, not much is known about Levi. He threw a party...and wrote a wonderful gospel. Yet, what can we really know about this disciple that Jesus chose to name Matthew? Jesus saw something in him, something that when redeemed and refined by Jesus, would be useful and productive for the Kingdom. Matthew was apparently an excellent accountant and record keeper. The gospel that bears his name confirms that fact. Matthew was drawn to the details, and Jesus needed someone just like that for his ministry. Those who knew Levi as the tax collector, and despised him for it, likely found Levi's new name puzzling. Who, but Jesus, would think that a tax collector was a "gift from God," yet that is what the name Matthew means. It is also likely that Matthew was the most educated, as well as the wealthiest, of those first disciples. It could also be true that Matthew had a brother who was also a disciple of Jesus. In Mark 2:14, Matthew is referenced as the son of Alphaeus. As we will discover there was another disciple, James the Less, who was also referred to as the son of Alphaeus. If this Alphaeus mentioned by Mark is one and the same with the one associated with James, then Matthew and James (the less) were brothers.

Who but Jesus would reach into the ranks of the publicans and pull out a tax collector by the name of Levi and make him an apostle? Matthew's job was lucrative, but it was certainly not an enviable position. He had to come farther, had to give up more, and perhaps had to confess more wrongs than any other apostle. Tax collectors were called publicans, which comes from a Latin term meaning public servant. They were an extension of the greedy hand of Rome. To succeed as a publican, one had to be shrewd, scheming and typically dishonest. Levi seems to have adapted well to that world of politics, which disguised itself as public service.

Jesus, however, saw something about Matthew that could be redeemed for Kingdom business rather than the business of Rome. His ability to keep up with the data and the details would be useful in preparing a written record (gospel) of the life of Christ.

Matthew's position of tax collector was well suited to his choleric temperament. He possessed strong willpower and effective leadership skills. The Lord was able to capture those qualities, transform them by grace, and use that same driving force as an asset.

HIS PROFESSION

Matthew had chosen a detested profession. He had grown up with a keen mind and a cleverness that led him to think that money talks. Matthew's desire was to make money so that he could have the good things in life. He wanted respect and he felt that money alone could get that respect. In the profession of tax gathering he saw an opportunity to make money, and apparently it did not matter to him that he was a Jew working for Rome. It was that fact, however, that caused Matthew to be detested by his fellow Jews. The Jewish underground, known as the Sicarii (dagger men), looked for opportunities to assassinate Romans, and those who affiliated with the Romans. One would think that Matthew may have very well been an intended target for the Sicarii. As is discovered later in this book, it appears that Jesus had recruited at least one hot-headed Jew who likely belonged to the underground group.

Palestine had fallen into hands of Alexander and the Greeks, and after the Romans conquered Greece, the Roman Empire swallowed up the Jewish nation. The Greek and Latin languages and customs influenced Jewish life. Among the many changes demanded by the Romans the tribute (tax) demanded by the government was among the most irksome things to the Jews. They felt that they owed God, and God alone, any tribute that was going to be paid.

It appears that Matthew located his collection booth in a very strategic place along a great highway that ran from Babylon, down into Egypt and all the way around the Mediterranean world. A branch of that road led off into Galilee to the city of Capernaum. By locating there Matthew could see every fishing boat with its catch and see every traveler on the road on their way to Greece. With the full authority of Rome, he could tax them all and therefore, he quickly became an enemy of the Jews.

Clearly, Matthew had chosen a detested profession. As an especially detested person he was seen as a sinner, leading us to recall that the Jews spoke of publicans and sinners as one and the same. Publicans were said to be disloyal to God and to the heritage of Israel. They were therefore sinners in the eyes of all Jews. Of course, in Matthew's case his love of money drove him to the profession, and as a result Matthew was looked upon as a leech in in his own culture and society.

Matthew also became a social outcast. He was cut off from all people, including family and those who had once been friends. His professional decisions had made him a pariah and there was not a loyal Jew in all of Israel who would pay Matthew the least of courtesies. He was not welcome in the synagogue or in other public gathering places. He was shunned like a leper and avoided like a thief. Socially he was in the same class with prostitutes.

As a tax gatherer Matthew was also considered a traitor, a betrayer of the nation. His "kind" was regarded as renegades from the national faith and the great Messianic hope. His kinsman writhed under the tyranny and oppression of Rome, and when he went to work for Rome his love for country was clearly overpowered by greed and a desire for some semblance of power.

Matthew had also chosen a disreputable profession that used the authority of Rome to prey on average citizens. There were two types of taxes and tax collectors in the Roman system of Matthew's day. The "Gabbai" collected the statutory taxes. There was also the "Mokhes" tax collector, who was more like a customs officer. Doubtless Levi had been called a thief, robber, and crook by those from whom he collected taxes. Everyone knew this profession, which had the protection of a corrupt government, to be dishonest. The Romans had a set amount of tax to be collected, and any amount collected above that amount mandated by Rome was kept by the tax men. They collected the money, kept their own records and Rome did not care how much they collected beyond the amount deemed due to Rome. Fifteen per cent was the usual the minimum and some tax collectors charged as much as twenty-five per cent. Most customs men (tax collectors) were regarded as criminals, who could do as they wished with full backing from Rome. Most of the publicans could look at a person and "size them up" and determine how much tax they could pay. They would often use their position as tax collector to also lend money, of course at exorbitant rates of interest. The job of tax collector was awarded to the highest bidder at an auction, with the high bidder getting the job. It was from such an unlikely profession that Jesus found a follower.

Tax collecting was a destructive profession as well. Truly, the only friend that a tax collector had was another tax collector. After getting the job it was easy for graft, fraud, greed, and extortion to take over a man's life. Matthew's integrity was soon destroyed. Matthew had likely made more money than he could spend, but to his dismay the satisfaction he had sought still eluded him.

Even family relationships had been destroyed by Matthew's job. His entire family would have suffered from the pain of ostracism directed toward Matthew. Even the children in the streets knew him as a publican and treated him in a demeaning manner. The only friends a publican had were the other publicans. He had sold his conscience and his faith for personal gain. Matthew was a walking dead man, for his honor had been sold and his conscience had been seared. His great heritage was sold for the custom seat. It has been said that the worst thing about wealth is that it costs so much. That was certainly the truth for Matthew.

HIS PROFOUND CHANGE

The change which occurred in Matthew's life came about first because of a direct request from Jesus. Matthew had probably seen and heard Jesus long before his personal encounter with Him. It was while Matthew sat at the collection table that Jesus approached him and challenged him to "Follow me."

The challenge of "Follow me" was the simple request of the Lord. It was a request for Matthew to leave his job. His job was giving him wealth but no satisfaction. Now there came this request to forsake it all and follow after Christ, without the guarantee of any income. There can be no doubt that Jesus had observed Matthew in the tax booth and had already observed those qualities that could benefit the Kingdom. In Matthew, the Lord saw a man hungry for peace and satisfaction, the kind only Jesus himself could give. To Matthew went the invitation to become a collector of souls rather than a collector of money. It was an invitation to trade "bosses." The thing of note in all of this is that Jesus' invitation was not predicated on who or what Matthew was, or what he had to offer Jesus. Jesus invitation was extended to a guy who was dishonest, greedy, had not been in the synagogue since who knows when, and a fellow who was rudely treated by any and all who knew him. Matthew did nothing. Jesus took him just like he was. You see, that is how Jesus works. He takes our worst and transforms it into his best. The Bible says that in Christ we are made new creatures. That was the offer of Jesus to Matthew.

That transformation, that new life, the filling of his once empty soul with purpose and meaning, was now awaiting nothing but the response of Matthew. Had he not responded, he would have passed up the opportunity to know the Prince of Peace. It must have been a great challenge for Matthew to decide what to do. The tables meant prosperity, but Christ meant peace. It was Matthew's decision: keep doing what he had always done with those same outcomes, or choose to follow Jesus. We can only imagine Matthew's inner conflict in that precise moment. It must have been a great battle of conscience and conviction. He could remain at his table and grow even more wealthy, or he could follow Jesus and discover riches that money cannot buy. Matthew chose to follow Christ. Matthew had no idea of what would be required of him, but at that point in his life it did not really matter. He was ready for change; he knew that even with money and protection from the Romans, his life was empty. Matthew was convinced that there was not another person who could help him. The gospel writer Luke says that when Matthew responded to Jesus' call that he left all and followed Him. There was no hesitation or reservation on the part of Matthew. When the call came, he readily responded to Jesus.

Because of the profound change in Matthew's life, there was great rejoicing. For the first time in many years there was a sense of peace and joy in his life. He had been delivered from the power of sin and he wanted the whole world to know it. Matthew went home and prepared a feast and invited Jesus and a number of other tax collectors to attend the feast; after all, those were the only folks that would show up at his house. Matthew wanted the men he had worked with to be present when he publicly announced his faith in the Lord.

Many a person has attempted to reform their life. Obviously, some have been more successful than others. However, reformation is never enough. Real change, lasting change, requires transformation. Transformation is the work of Jesus Christ. When Matthew accepted the invitation of Jesus to, *"Follow me,"* his life was transformed. Transformation begins at the point of salvation. Jesus said in Matthew 11:28-29, *"Come to me, all who labor and are heavy laden, and I will give you rest. Take my yoke upon you , and learn from me, for I am gentle and lowly in heart, and you will find rest for your souls."* The Message Bible says it this way, *"Are you tired? Worn out? Burned out on religion? Come to me. Get away with me and you'll recover your life. I'll show you how to take a real rest. Walk with me and work with me – watch how I do it. Learn the unforced rhythms of grace. I won't lay anything heavy or ill-fitting on you. Keep company with me and you'll learn to live freely and lightly."* Wow! Can you imagine what Matthew thought and felt when he first heard Jesus say those words? The apostle Paul told us *"...the free gift of God is eternal life in Jesus Christ our Lord."* Paul also said, *"For everyone who calls on the name of the Lord will be saved"* (Romans 10:13). How can that be true? Again, Paul in Romans 10 states, *"If you confess with your mouth that Jesus is Lord, and believe in your heart that God raised him from the dead, you will be saved."* Matthew's profound change began the day he said yes to Jesus.

Matthew was not only saved, but he was also sanctified. I believe that sanctification is both positional and progressive. The term sanctify simple means "to be set apart." I, like Matthew, had a change in position the day I trusted Jesus to save me. It's simple - when I called on Jesus to forgive and save me - my position changed from lost (sinful, imperfect) to found (saved, redeemed). I certainly did not become perfect. As the old hymn says I am "prone to wander." Yet, as I obey 1 John 1:9, forgiveness comes again and again, and as I abide in Christ (stay close) I am forgiven and renewed. That is what I mean by progressive sanctification. John 17: 9-19 is a great reminder of how Jesus, knowing what we confront each day in the world, is praying (interceding) for us. In verse 19 Jesus said, *"I consecrate myself, that they also may be sanctified in truth."*

I am a Rotarian, and our motto – known around the world – is "Service Above Self." This profound change in Matthew's life also led him to a place where he came to understand that the Christ-life is one that places service above self. The Christ life begins when we act upon the words of Jesus, *"follow me."* Mark 2:14 tells of that day Matthew heard those words from Jesus, and the verse goes on to say, *"...and he arose and followed him."* From that point forward, Matthew was never the same.

HIS PROFITABLE LIFE

To Matthew privilege meant responsibility. A person is never saved without a purpose and without that person having a place of service to fill. Matthew saw to it that his life counted for Jesus.

Matthew, the once dishonest tax collector, became an honest witness for Christ. From the feast he gave when other publicans were invited, right to the very end of his life, Matthew presented a witness for the Lord. He could think of no better witness than to let those who had known him see the difference in his life. He learned that his purpose in life was not to make a profit for himself, but to make himself profitable for the Kingdom of God. That he did by being a consistent witness for the Lord. Now rather than collecting tribute for the Empire of Rome, he began collecting transformed sinners for the Kingdom of heaven.

Matthew's life was also profitable to Christ as he served as a humble apostle. He possessed a humility which enabled him to lose sight of himself and serve Jesus without a hint of reservation. As Matthew records the names of the apostles in his gospel, he includes the fact that he was a publican. This served as a reminder that he was a debtor to Christ. He was not proud of the past, but he never wanted to forget or overlook that he was a sinner saved by the grace of Jesus Christ.

Matthew has little to say about his experiences among the other apostles. He wanted only that his readers might see Jesus Christ in all that had taken place in his life.

Matthew proved to be profitable to Christ as an honorable writer. As a writer he kept very accurate and precise records from his experiences with Christ. He remembered and wrote some things that escaped the notice of the other writers. It was Matthew who remembered that Jesus said, "*You can't serve God and money.*" Those words possibly spoke to no one as they did to Matthew. He had spent a long time trying to serve the world and to make money, get rich. He found that he was left empty and alone with his money. Matthew is also the one who remembered that Jesus said, "*But seek first the Kingdom of God, and His righteousness; and all these things will be added to you.*"

Matthew's gospel was written around 70 A.D., and he met the need in early Christian life for a record of the life of Christ. As churches multiplied and the apostles passed away, the eyewitnesses were called upon to recall the past. Matthew wrote basically from a Jewish perspective and his gospel proves his familiarity with Jewish tradition, Scripture, and history.

Matthew's changed life stands for all the ages to know that Jesus died for the outcast of society, and that Jesus has the desire and the power to save all who turn, by faith, to him.

4

ANDREW: APOSTLE OF FERVENCY

A ndrew was, of course, Simon Peter's brother. In most cases
when he is mentioned in the Bible he is referred to as "Simon
Peter's brother." Peter was the outspoken leader of the group while
Andrew was quieter, seeming to prefer working in the background.
Andrew was the first to receive an invitation from Jesus, as is
recorded in John's gospel. Andrew and John had become disciples
of John the Baptist, and it was while standing next to the Baptist, as
Jesus walked by, they heard John say, *"Behold the Lamb of God!"* The
two disciples of the Baptist immediately started following Jesus, and
they were so obvious that Jesus turned to them and said, *"What are
you seeking?*

Their reply to Jesus came in the form of a question, *"Where are
you staying?"*

"Come and you will see," said Jesus.

I readily admit that I am always captivated by what John 1:39
records next. The Bible says, *"So they came and saw where he was staying,
and they stayed with him that day...."*

Oh, wow! What an incredible experience that must have been,
an entire day with Jesus. I spend time with Jesus every day, and I
always leave amazed, refreshed and energized. Of course, my time

with Jesus is courtesy of the Holy Spirit…and mind you that is no small thing. Yet, Andrew was invited, by Jesus himself to, as the country folk I grew up with would say, "Come in a sit a spell." What could be more captivating and transforming than such an experience? Andrew was never the same again, and just think, the day is fast approaching when all of us as believers will receive that same invitation to "Come in and see." For us it will not be to spend the day, rather to spend eternity in the company of Jesus.

Along with Peter, James and John, there is considerable evidence to suggest that Andrew was a part of the so-called inner circle of Jesus. Of those four disciples we know the least about Andrew. Peter, James and John are sort of the "Big Three," simply because their personalities trended toward a more vocal, visible and dominant style. Mark's gospel in 1:29 and 13:3 connects Andrew to the inner circle. Some, while working in the background, will allow jealousy and envy to rob them of the joy of their involvement in the Lord's work. That seems to have never been an issue for Andrew. It is interesting that when we find Andrew, we also find a group of people. This perhaps suggests that Andrew was a warm, friendly and compassionate person. As a social style, it may be that the amiable style best describes Andrew. The amiable social style person tends to be friendly, supportive and relationship oriented. That would also make Andrew a phlegmatic individual, described therefore as quiet, easy going and sympathetic. If we could have Andrew complete the DISC Theory personality inventory, I think he would the poster-boy for the "S" personality type (steady, loyal, team focused). Andrew is only mentioned fourteen times in the Bible, yet there was something amazing, something special about him. Andrew had a zeal, a fervency for Christ that not many possess. Dare we be such fervent disciples of Jesus? Dare we not?

ANDREW'S CHARACTERISTICS

Andrew's reputation was clearly that of a devout and religious man. He appears to have been well versed in the Jewish faith, and the Bible clearly shows us that Andrew was making regular trips into the desert to hear John the Baptist preach. When we first meet Andrew, he was a long way from his hometown of Bethsaida, which is in the region of Galilee. Like his brother Peter, he had relocated to Capernaum, and along with Peter, James and John they made many trips to the desert to hear the Baptist. Clearly, they were paying attention to the sermons, especially those mentions regarding the long-awaited arrival of Messiah.

Andrew was not only devout in his faith, he also proved to be incredibly dependable. Any pastor reading this book will agree with me when I say that every pastor looks for those individuals within the church who can be counted on through thick and thin. Every leader has found an abundance of people willing to attach themselves to the minister and the ministry when all is well. Without exception, sooner or later, something will happen, or some person will grumble, and at that juncture the many become the few, relative to issues of dependability. Oh, that every church could be filled with many Andrew's, especially as it relates to the marvelous testimony the Bible shares with us about him, *"Andrew first found his brother...."* Jesus' initial call to potential disciples was, *"Follow me and I will make you fishers of men."* Andrew caught on fast! I can assure you, Andrew never stopped introducing people to Jesus. What a testimony, what a legacy.

Whatever characteristics Jesus was looking for as he made choices for those early disciples, Andrew was certainly well qualified. The word "disciple" simply means a follower and a learner. In many ways those first disciples are to be envied. They had a first-hand, intimate, close encounter of the spiritual kind with Jesus. Earlier we observed that on the first day that Andrew met Jesus they spent the entire day together. Now, Andrew gets to spend every day with Jesus. You will have to excuse me for a moment, having thought about Andrew's experience with Jesus, and relating that to my own experience with Jesus, I feel a song welling up in my soul...

Every day with Jesus is sweeter than the day before,
Every day with Jesus I love him more and more.

Andrew and the other disciples were invited to an intimate relationship with Jesus. Can that sort of bond be replicated today? In one way, no. No, simply because we are temporarily distanced from Jesus by space. He is "there," and we are "here." However, because we have something and someone those first disciples did not have, that is the abiding presence of the Holy Spirit, we too can have an ongoing, intimate, relationship with Jesus Christ. Jesus made that very clear for us in John 15:1-11. Within that section of the Bible he said, *"Abide in me, and I in you...I am the vine, you are the branches. Whoever abides in me and I in him, he it is that bears much fruit, for apart from me you can do nothing.... These things have I spoken to you, that my joy may be in you, that your joy may be full."* So yes, we can enjoy that same intimate relationship with Jesus that Andrew and the others experienced. As we worship, as we pray, as we read and mediate on the Word of God...Jesus is present. That is exactly what Jesus had in mind when he said, *"Abide in me, and I in you."*

ANDREW'S CONVERSION

As stated earlier, Andrew was captivated by the preaching of John the Baptist, and the day John said (my translation) "Look, that's the Messiah who has come to save the world," Andrew knew he had found the One he had been expecting. Perhaps Andrew even saw something majestic about the stride of Jesus as he walked down the street. Andrew, perhaps, even though a devout Jew, had begun to sense that his spiritual needs were no longer being met by the ceremonies and rituals of his religion. Perhaps the teaching of the Scribes and Pharisees seemed a mere formality, void of any relationship to Andrew's current reality. John's gospel confirms that on that glad day when Andrew and John—yes, John the writer of the gospel, first met Jesus, they followed him. Jesus extended an invitation, *"Come and see,"* their acceptance of that invitation forever changed their lives. You see, when we follow Jesus, transformation occurs. Life is never again the same. Following Jesus means redemption, as though we were bought from an enslaved life, and set free in Christ. Following Jesus means passing from death to life.

Following Jesus means no more condemnation. Following Jesus means we have been justified (made right) by faith. Following Jesus means we have peace with God, and perhaps for the first time, we have hope. Following Jesus means that we have been reconciled (a once severed relationship is now restored) with God. As a young boy I belonged to a missions group called Royal Ambassadors. We had a hymn we sang that declared we were ambassadors for the King in a foreign land. The chorus to that hymn is something I have never forgotten…

> This is the message that I bring, a message angels
>   fain would sing: Oh be ye reconciled, thus saith
>   my Lord and King, Oh be ye reconciled to God.

Indeed!

Here are a few observations regarding the conversion of Andrew that I found true of my own conversion:

- His conversion was personal - We have already seen Andrew follow Jesus to where he was staying. All relationships with Jesus begin on the personal level. Even those who are converted while attending church or some mass meeting, it remains true: heart to heart is how we all began our relationship with Jesus.
- His conversion was permanent - It seems that Andrew died on an X shaped cross sometime around 69 AD. From the moment of his "new birth," until the day he died, there is nothing to suggest that Andrew ever faltered in his faith. Furthermore, Andrew had been there on that day Jesus said, *"I will never leave or forsake you."* I am certain Andrew found those words completely trustworthy.
- His conversion was purposeful - Goodness, was it ever! Andrew was an integral component of Jesus' strategy to ensure that everyone had the opportunity to hear the good news…Jesus saves! I am particularly fond of this

Old Testament Scripture, for it contains the most basic concept of Gods purpose and requirement for each of us as believers. *"He has told you, O man, what is good, and what does the Lord require of you but to do justice, and to love kindness, and to walk humbly with your God."* (Micah 6:8) Andrew's conversion met that requirement, and more.

ANDREW'S CALL

Take a moment to think…what do you suppose to be life's greatest question? There are plenty of contenders for the answer. Who am I? Where did I come from, and where am going? What is the meaning of life, why am I here? Is there life in outer space? Heavy duty sort of questions, don't you agree? On the lighter side it might be the old question of which came first, the chicken or the egg? Seriously, what is your answer?

For Andrew, life's greatest question spoken directly to him is recorded in John 1:38, *"What are you seeking?"* Wow, some question. It's one most of us have likely asked ourselves. What do I want out of life? What am I seeking? That question confronts all of us. Sadly, many of the answers we provide lead down the wrong path. Wrong answers include addictions, suicides, harmful habits, excesses, neglect, negative thoughts and hundreds of such answers. Andrew's answer resulted in spending an entire day with Jesus, which led to his subsequent answer to the simple statement of Jesus, *"Follow me."* It was at that point that Andrew laid aside what he had been doing, and did just as Jesus asked. Andrew followed Jesus.

Andrew's response came because he had experienced life's great moment. That moment for Andrew is defined in the Bible with these simple words, *"They came and saw…."* What was it that Andrew, along with John, saw? The words of Jesus, *"Come and see,"* and the response that followed, *"They came and saw,"* defines the width and the depth of any person's relationship with Jesus. That moment when we hear, with our spiritual ears, the invitation of Jesus, and our response mirrors that of Andrew, in that moment we have made the most important decision of our life.

Matthew 4: 18-20 records what was, and is, life's greatest response. His response would demand of him tremendous sacrifices. The life of a missionary and church planter is filled with demands, difficulties and often danger. Andrew said yes to the call of Jesus.

ANDREW'S COMMITMENT

Commitment to such a life, such a calling, requires a firm foundation. Andrew spent three years training and preparing for his assignment. In both attitude and accomplishments, we can confirm that Andrew was well prepared for his assignment. In Ephesians 2: 18-20 Paul the apostle declares that we, as Christians, have access to our heavenly Father through the Holy Spirit, and because we do, we are not strangers and aliens within the household of God. Then verse twenty makes this statement, confirming the place of Andrew and the other apostles, in the household of God, "...*built on the foundation of the apostles and prophets, Christ Jesus himself being the cornerstone....*" Don't miss that! This household, this Kingdom, to which we belong stands strong because its foundation is strong. Andrew's name means "manly," "strong," "brave," "courageous," and "warrior." Strong indeed!

We need more Andrews in the modern church. Why? Andrew was the first identifiable soul winner, seeking out his own brother in order to introduce him to Christ. It was Andrew in John chapter six who stood next to Jesus with the lad's five loaves and two fish and had the faith that that small lunch would feed more than 5,000 people. In John 12:20-22 a group of Greeks approached Philip, who was also an apostle, and said, "*We wish to see Jesus.*" What happened next is such a revelation regarding the character and heart of Andrew. Philip took the Greeks to Andrew. Did you ever wonder why Philip did not just take them to Jesus rather than taking them to Andrew? I believe Andrew was among the inner circle of Jesus, but that is not the reason. Andrew was transparent, and Philip as well as the other apostles well knew Andrew was passionate about introducing people to Jesus. Oh, if we were only more passionate about making introductions to Jesus, what a better world we would live in today.

There are many stories and much tradition surrounding the travels and ministry of Andrew. It may be that he ministered in Asia Minor and in Bithynia, which became the location of the Nicean Council in 325 AD. There is much which cannot be confirmed, but there is an absolute truth. Andrew never stopped looking for the next person he could introduce to Jesus. When was the last time you deliberately talked to someone about Jesus?

5

SIMON: THE APOSTLE WHO FOUGHT

S imon is recognized in Scripture as Simon the Zealot or Simon the Cananite, not to be confused with Canaan in Galilee. The title which has been attached to his name reveals a great deal about his temperament. Zealot means that he was an aggressive patriot who was given to fighting. He had grown weary of the Roman yoke and had chosen to take up arms against them. The style employed by the Zealots was a guerrilla type warfare. He has been called the "Patrick Henry of the Apostles." A Zealot is most surely of the choleric temperament. The choleric personality type would be a person of strong willpower, perhaps a leader, and often hot-tempered and impetuous. Simon's social style was a vivid combination of driver and expressive. Jesus already had one Simon who was impetuous and would require a lot of work. Now he had two of them. The work that Jesus did in the life of Simon Zealotes is evidence of what Jesus can do with an undisciplined, destructive personality by transforming it into a powerful force for Kingdom work.

The term "Cananaean" has been attached to the name of Simon. Some have wrongly taken that as a reference to the town of Cana as the birthplace of Simon. However, that is not the meaning of the word at all. Cananaean comes from "Kana" which means to be ardent or zealous. Simon was a member of a revolutionary party among the Jews called the Zealots.

The Greek name Zealot is the only thing the Bible tells us about Simon. Yet that one word is enough to describe the zeal and enthusiasm with which he operated, and a characteristic that appealed to Jesus as he considered the need for disciples with great energy, commitment, loyalty and enthusiasm. Not a single word or deed that Simon said or did is recorded in Scripture. It is from that one little word, Zealot, that a character sketch of Simon is made.

Few of the individuals that Jesus chose as disciples would make it past the first interview by any business owners I have known. Certainly, no CEO would take a chance on Simon. Yet here he is on the team.

It is equally difficult to try to determine why Simon chose to follow Jesus. Was it because the Zealots lacked leadership? Was it a sermon he had heard Jesus preach? Did he see in Christ the Messiah that he likely heard John the Baptist talk about so often? Was it that Simon thought this Messiah would himself be a Zealot who would lead them to victory over the Romans? It may be that Simon chose to follow Jesus with the expectation of political victory and the hope of freedom. One can see how Simon would be attracted to Jesus, but it becomes more difficult to understand why Jesus would choose one like Simon.

Ponder this…if you could select only one word by which you would still be known hundreds of years after you passed on from this life…what would it be? For Simon the word is Zealot, basically a political party. I don't want the name of any political party to be how I am remembered. What word would communicate your interests, your loyalties, your abilities? The day will come when folks stand and look at our tombstone and some word will pop into their mind. For now, we can help them come up with that word. What will that word be that defines you?

SIMON'S ENTHUSIAM

Simon was certainly a very enthusiastic man, especially when it came to expressing his loyalties to the people and causes that mattered most to him. He was enthusiastic about his country. He was a patriot of patriots. The party of the Zealots dates back to the time of the Maccabees, a time that seemed to call for making a stand against foreign influences that were disrupting Jewish religious life. Those early patriots banded together under Judas of Samala to attempt to remove the region of Judea from Roman domination. They were fanatical Jews who were very vocal in their declaration that Rome had destroyed the independence of Israel, and had made it impossible for Jews observe and practice their religious ceremonies. The Zealots made their headquarters in Galilee and made it their business to stir up sedition and rebellion at every opportunity. Acts 5:37 refers to one known as Judas the Galilean. This individual was, like Simon, an individual that loathed Roman rule over the land of the Jews. Judas the Galilean led an insurrection against the Roman government for requiring Jews to participate in a census, the very census that causes Mary and Joseph to travel and arrive in Bethlehem just in time for the birth of Jesus. Judas the Galilean was eventually killed for his efforts within the Zealots. He, along with many Jews, envisioned Israel as a theocracy. Theocracy refers to the rule of God. Several of the so-called religious/political parties of the day felt a responsibility only to God. He alone was to be obeyed and anyone else who sought to bring them into bondage was to be resisted. For the strict Jew, God was the only King. Therefore, to the Zealot the war against Rome was not a political uprising; rather, it was a holy war.

The other dominant political parties of that period included the Pharisees, the Sadducees, the Essenes and the Zealots. All of them had opposed the Roman rule, but the Zealots were...well, zealous in their opposition.

Herod the Great had died in 4 B.C., at which time his region of power was divided among his three sons. The division of Israel brought outcries from the Israelites. The Romans inflicted a universal taxation on all Jews and that exacerbated the growing unrest. They rebelled against paying tribute (tax) to anyone except God, and the thought of worshipping Caesar was even more repugnant. We have already seen how Levi, himself a Jew, had become a pawn of Rome and a pariah among his own people. From that boiling cauldron of animosity and resistance came the Zealots. They were a particularly ardent group, and among their members there arose a number of them who became known as the "Sicarii" or the "Assassins." Under their outer coat they carried a dagger, ready to fight and murder as deemed necessary for their cause of freedom. Their fanaticism turned into sheer madness. They willingly became arresting officer, prosecutor, judge, jury and executioner – all, with one swipe of the blade. Simon and his companions did what they did in the name of their country. Be sure of this: Simon loved his country and was ready to die for her. Thus, he and his zealous friends had no hesitation, and no regrets, for their murderous activity.

While I cannot support the methodology of Simon's zeal relative to his love for country, his zeal does make me grieve over the loss of some of our patriotism here in America. We burn the flag of our country, we denounce the brave men and women who serve in the military, we tolerate abuse, and denigrate our policemen and policewomen. We kill the unborn with impunity. The glory of our nation has been surrendered to the greedy and the self-serving who have become the embodiment of Psalm 52:3, *"You love evil more than good, and lying more than speaking what is right."* Somewhere in this story about Simon and his zeal for his country, there rises in me something far beyond nostalgia. For the here and now I long for our nation to kneel before our true King, for the Bible says, *"Blessed is the nation whose God is the Lord"* (Psalm 33:12). At the same time may I never forget what Jesus said, *"My Kingdom is not of this world..."* (John 18:36). Paul reminded the Ephesians that we all *"...were by nature children of wrath...but God, being rich in mercy...made us alive with Christ... by grace you have been saved."*

Not only was Simon enthusiastic about his country, but he was also enthusiastic about Christ. Simon had been fighting for deliverance, now he had found personal deliverance in Jesus Christ. A mighty transformation had taken place in his life. That life changing moment came through amazing grace, grace found in Jesus and his message. Simon's fiery zeal was refined and refined again, until at last it was made into a lasting zeal for Jesus Christ and the new Kingdom. Simon left the fanatical control of Judas the Galilean and followed another Galilean, one who said, *"My yoke is easy."*

There is no Biblical indication as to how Jesus and Simon first met, or what was said or done. However, there can be no question that the Lord saw in him an individual who matched exactly the demands of an ambassador for Christ. No doubt, Simon served the Lord faithfully and took his share of the missionary work alongside the other twelve. He left a party of insurrectionists for the Prince of Peace. Simon recognized that Jesus was the true prince and Messiah of Israel. Though he may have been attracted by the thought of an overthrow to be led by Jesus, he quickly learned that the kingdom of Jesus was not of this world. It was no minor miracle when Simon left his party for the company of the twelve.

It is important to note that even after Simon was called to be an apostle, he never ceased to be called a Zealot. The political enthusiasm that he had was refined and surely carried over into his relationship with Jesus. There can be little doubt that as he worked and witnessed as an apostle, he did so with zeal and enthusiasm. I must believe that Simon became an enthusiastic learner (disciple) and missionary (apostle). Simon was one who was willing to surrender himself completely to Jesus. Many would not have considered Simon a candidate for apostleship, but Jesus looked beyond the outward anger of a man intent on mayhem, and even murder. Jesus saw what was, but more importantly, he saw what could be, and in fact was done through the transformed life of a zealot. Only Jesus could reach into such a dangerous class of underground fighters and find one suitable to be one of the master's men. As we are beginning to learn, the apostles represent every element of society. The Lord turns His back on no one who is willing to honestly answer the call of Jesus. Simon has been described as a trophy of what divine grace can do and perhaps in some ways became the forerunner of another rebel, who one day, while in a ditch beside the road to Damascus, was confronted and transformed by Christ. Simon and all the others are evidence of what can be done when one yields totally Jesus Christ.

HIS EMERGENCE

Each of the apostles emerges into what Christ envisioned for them, after all, God has an eternal design for each of us. Each apostle had to emerge from something and into something. Before his encounter with Christ, Simon was concerned only with his own ambitions and personal interests. His primary focus was his political interests, and to that he devoted all his time. However, all that changed when Jesus entered his life. Suddenly those other disciples of Jesus, serving alongside Simon, became an increasingly important part of his life. Such is the church for us. The joy of serving alongside others of kindred hearts is matched by few things in our lives. For us, as it was for Simon, finds all that other "stuff" becoming less important, for after all we are here on Kingdom assignment. No longer was a political party the most important thing to Simon, but instead he became a lover of the souls of men. Simon emerged out of his private world of political aspirations to become an apostle of the Lord Jesus Christ.

Most important, Simon emerged out of his sin. He and his associates preyed upon and took advantage of other people. The Zealots would attack a village and then take the spoils of their plundering. Immorality was a common mark of the Zealots. Life was cheap in the world of a Zealot, and murder, when deemed necessary by their own politically motivated aspirations, was common. The Zealots made a target any Roman official, and they saw any Roman property as fair game for stealing. They were even willing to kill any Jew who seemed to favor or compromise with Rome. The entire ugly mess came to a head in 70 AD. People were starving, civil war had broken out in Jerusalem and the Zealots were terrorizing the city. It was this mad mess that led to the Roman destruction of Jerusalem. Masada, which ended with 966 deaths (killings and suicides) became their last stand. Only two women and five children survived this ancient version of Waco. It was out of all this ugliness that Simon was called by Jesus and enlisted in a new kind of army, an army with different armor and different weapons (Ephesians 6:13-20; 2 Corinthians 10:3-6), fighting a much more insidious enemy, Satan himself. (Ephesian 6:10-12). Such a reminder brings us to a personal hallelujah moment…Jesus is able to reach to the lowest depths to save the soul of anyone who in faith and repentance, calls His name. Romans 10:13 says, *"For everyone who calls on the name of the Lord will be saved."* I am certain that Simon was grateful for the inclusion of the word, *everyone.* I am so thankful that "everyone" included me, how about you? No matter our past, or the depth of our sin, we remain among those Jesus came to transform.

From selfishness and sin, Simon emerged a servant of the Lord. An apostle is one who is sent. Simon accepted the challenge to be a fisher of men and to go wherever the Lord sent Him. Simon could never be the kind of man who would approach anything halfheartedly. That was simply not his personality. We can be most certain that he was all in…100% for the Lord. By faith he followed Christ and by faith he never looked back. Simon exchanged the party of war for the prince of peace. He exchanged a life filled with hatred for a life filled with hope. He exchanged a life of fighting for a life of faith. He exchanged a loveless life for a life of eternal love.

HIS ETERNAL LOVE

Goodness, how does one go from being a likely murderer, an insurrectionist, to a disciple and apostle of the Son of God? Simon found an inner peace that had long evaded him. He belonged to an underground, terrorist-like organization. He had been angry at the world, he had despised his fate, his soul burned with anger. Now, however, his heart was gripped by a peace that he never imagined possible. From where had that peace come? The answer is simple: Jesus. Who but Christ could put a tax hater like Simon the Zealot and a tax collector like Matthew the publican together? Outside their common relationship with Jesus, those two were mortal enemies. We have one guy who got his paycheck from Rome, and a second guy who wanted Rome destroyed.

It was this inner peace that led to the great love that Simon possessed. It was great love because it was the love of Christ in him. The love of Jesus brought Simon together with those he hated and bonded and knit them into a great evangelistic team. Jesus is the God of *"Whosoever will, may come."*

Following the Roman execution of Jesus there were those who likely expected Simon to return to his radical ways among the Zealots, but in the words of an old gospel chorus I dearly love, Simon must have been true to his calling, singing along the way, *"We've come this far by faith, leaning on the Lord, trusting in His word, he's never failed me yet…can't turn around…"*

Tradition has Simon traveling with Jude, to Persia, Africa, Egypt and the British Isles. Simon's ministry was never about where, it was about who. The who was always Jesus. Simon had clearly adopted the message of John the Baptist, *"He must increase, but I must decrease"* (John 3:30).

6

JAMES (ALPHAEUS): APOSTLE OF LITTLE FAME

James, son of Alphaeus, is often called "the Less," some supposing it to be an indication of his height. Others say it refers to his seeming insignificance in the Bible and his apparent lack of leadership ability. Although everything that James said or did seems to have gone unnoticed, unheralded and unrecorded, there is no hint that he was anything but faithful in fulfilling his calling as a disciple and apostle.

Even though this apostle is remembered only by his name, it must be said that Christ saw in him the ingredients for faithfulness and for becoming a world changer. To Jesus, James was certainly more than just a name. Jesus knew his personal worth and Kingdom value when he selected him as one of the original twelve.

The name James has its root in the name Jacob and was a favorite name in New Testament times. There are at least four different men in the New Testament with this same name. Author H.S. Vigeveno says this James represents the unknown, of the numberless ones, of the nameless millions who follow Christ. He represents those millions who have been scattered over the world spreading the gospel and yet whose names go unrecorded. For every general, there are ten thousand privates who diligently carry out commands; such a one was James, son of Alphaeus. Jesus passed over many with influence, power and wealth and called a man who was virtually unknown except to those family and friends who were closest to him.

HIS FAMILY

Perhaps a quick word about who he was not is in order:

- Our James was not James, the brother of John, the son of Zebedee.
- Our James was not James, the son of Mary and the half-brother of Jesus Christ. James, the son of Mary was never an apostle. James, son of Mary, did however, later in life become a disciple of Jesus and lived boldly for the Lord, became a pastor and wrote the book of James in the New Testament.
- Our James was not James, the father of Thaddaeus. Thaddaeus was also known as "Judas, not Iscariot."

So, who then was this James, the apostle of little fame?

- His father was Alphaeus, and Alphaeus is also known as Clopas in the Bible.
- His mother was Mary. Mary was a common name of those times, and is found multiple times in the Bible. As examples we know that the mother of James and John, the sons of Zebedee, was also named Mary. The most heralded Mary in the Bible is of course, the mother of Jesus. Then there was Mary Magdalene, one of the early disciples of Jesus. Of course, there were numerous others who shared the name Mary with these few examples.
- James, son of Alphaeus had a brother name Levi. In Mark 2:14 Levi is identified as the son of Alphaeus. Assuming this to be one and the same Alphaeus who was the father of James, Levi and James are indeed brothers.

- Many scholars believe that Mary, mother of Jesus, and Mary the mother of James, son of Alphaeus, were sisters. Mary, mother of James is identified in Mark 15:40 as being at the cross when Jesus died, and she is also noted as the mother of both James and Joses (Joseph, another common name). This would mean that James, son of Alphaeus and Mary, had two brothers, Levi and Joseph. It would also mean that he was a cousin of Jesus.

Think of the problems this family faced. One son was a black sheep, so obsessed with money that he was willing to get cash by selling out his country and collecting taxes for Rome. Then there is James, son of Alphaeus who appears to have associated himself with Simon and the Zealots, which we previously discussed. Many Bible scholars agree that James too was a Zealot. The second son attached himself to a fanatical right-wing movement which resorted to mayhem and murder to accomplish their goals. Alphaeus must have had a significant problem trying to contend with Levi, an employee of Rome, and James who hated Rome. The third son, Joses, was reportedly extremely conservative in his thinking. Imagine what that family dinner may have been...we can be assured that there were no "Leave it to Beaver" episodes in that house.

HIS FAITHFULNESS

James, son of Alphaeus, was chosen as an apostle by the Lord after a night in prayer. Though nothing is recorded about James, Jesus knew the past and the future, and clearly saw God-sized possibilities in James. James, like all the others, was sent to preach the gospel and to heal the sick. The Lord, reader of our hearts, knower of our intentions, knew that James could be relied upon to render faithful service to God. James likely never gave Jesus any serious reason to worry; after all, there is no record of a doubt (Thomas), a denial (Peter), and certainly no dubious plots (Judas). Perhaps he does represent that long line of disciples who faithfully served, but of whom no record has been kept. The fact that his name is in the list of apostles given in the book of Acts indicates he was faithful as a Christian witness following the resurrection of Jesus, and well beyond into the future.

Paul, in 1 Corinthians 1:26-29, gives us the pattern God uses in His search for disciples, both then and now. James was a perfect fit for the pattern.

> *"For consider your calling, brothers; not many of you were wise according to worldly standards, not many were powerful, not many were of noble birth. But God chose what is foolish in the world to shame the wise; God chose what is weak to shame the strong; God chose what is low and despised in the world, even things that are not, to bring to nothing things that are, so that no human being might boast in the presence of God."*

God is looking for ordinary folk who are ready and willing to move into a new dimension with God. As those Scriptures remind us, God is not as interested in our intellect, our influence or our importance (status) as He is our willingness to surrender our total selves. The power of God is seen in that great fact.

The plan of God is to take nobodies and make them somebodies; to take the foolish and weak and confound the world; to take the weak and confront the mighty; to take the base and conquer the great. Many examples of that plan, and its success, are found in the Bible and throughout history. From the Bible we surely know the story of David and the conquest of the giant Goliath. Many of us have faced our own version of Goliath, only to see God step into our lives and bring down the giants we have faced. There is also the story of Gideon, who said of himself, *"My family is the poorest in all the tribe of Manesseh."* Yet, with only three hundred soldiers Gideon won a war with the Midianites. Like the Midianites of old, who wanted to destroy the God of Israel, we still face those who are at war with us because of our beliefs and our faith in almighty God. May we have the courage of Gideon in waging spiritual warfare against the supplicants of so many gods that are foreign to our faith.

God's purpose in all this business is to *"bring to nothing the things that are."* Nothing can separate us from the love of God. No amount of adversity, no onslaught of the evil one, not even death itself, can separate us from God. Paul, in Romans 8: 38-39 said, *"For I am sure that neither death or life, nor angels nor rulers, nor things present nor things to come....will be able to separate us from the love of God."*

James was committed and faithful to the Lord and even though, to us at least, his life was lived in obscurity, his name is written in the halls of heaven. Never once did he complain that he was not in the forefront where all the glory was. He was willing to do all that he could for Jesus and then to let it go on unnoticed. He was not Peter who stamped his personality on the first church, nor John who left us with the Revelation and he was not a Paul whose footprints are scattered across the entirety of the New Testament. He was James, who saw something that needed to be done, did it, and did not wait for glory or accolades to come pouring in on him.

The lesson in all this is that there is work to be done for King Jesus and the Kingdom, and it must be done now. Every person, in every generation, has an assignment to which Jesus is calling them, and it is an assignment that must be done without the expectation of praise in return.

HIS FUTURE GLORY

The labors of James may have gone unrecorded, but they will not go unrewarded. The word "redemption" appears eleven times in the New Testament. Each time, it is a reference to that future time when we stand before the Lord. In 1 Corinthians 3:13 that time, that day of judgment for believers – judgment not of sin and salvation, but judgment of works after salvation – tells us this, *"Each one's works will become manifest, for the Day will disclose it, because it will be revealed...if it was built on the foundation it survives, and he will receive a reward."* In Hebrews 11:33-38 is what might be called the "honor-roll of the un-named." Their faith did not falter. They could have escaped the atrocities that befell many of them, but they understood that the deliverance offered by the world's crowd is always temporary. Their unwillingness to compromise subjected them to many horrors, including death. Hebrews 11:40 could easily have been the epithet on their gravestone, *"God provided something better…"*

Be certain of this: James understood that service is not a principle. Service is an action. We Christians believe in the idea of service, but the roll-up-your-sleeves kind of service done in the name of Jesus, and done without expecting anything in return, has slowly evaporated. I do know this, James the son of Alphaeus, also called James the less, has a crown awaiting him. If no other crowns, and I am certain there are, James will receive the "Crown of Life." Revelation 2:10 says, *"Be faithful unto death and I will give you the crown of life."* We, like James, will not be judged by the fame we acquired during our lives, we will be judged only by the faith we acted upon during our lives.

7

JAMES: THE APOSTLE WHO FISHED

James, the son of Zebedee, along with his brother John, was known as the Son of Thunder. This mark of identification appears to have been given to him by Jesus as an indication of his temperament. We have previously established that the name James, which is a derivative of the name Jacob, was a somewhat common name in Jewish culture at the time of the early New Testament narrative. This James is not to be confused with others in the Bible with the same name. There is James, son of Alphaeus and of course, Jesus had a half-brother named James. Here we are considering James, the son of Zebedee, brother of John, both of whom were business partners with Peter and Andrew. Interestingly, Jona of Bethsaida, who was the father of Peter and Andrew, was also a partner in that fishing business.

Along with Peter and John, James was a member of the inner circle of Jesus' associates. We also established in another chapter that Andrew was likely a fourth member of that inner circle. James was a fisherman by trade and worked alongside his father Zebedee and his brother John. His nickname was likely given to him because of his sometime tempestuous personality. As for personality traits, we can assume that James was hot tempered, intense, with perhaps had a bent toward the occasional violent outburst. Scripture provides evidence that James was not only aggressive, but that he was also a man who possessed an ambitious spirit. His ambitious spirit could very well have been passed along to him from his mother, Salome.

Clearly, we see throughout Bible history that God has been able to use those preachers, prophets and disciples who had a fiery personality. The first Great Awakening in America included sermons from the blazing tongues of Jonathan Edwards, George Whitefield, and Gilbert Tennent. The Wesley brothers were firebrands of the gospel. Who is not familiar with Charles Spurgeon, A.W. Tozer, Billy Sunday and Billy Graham? From Scripture more examples include Elijah, Nehemiah, John the Baptist, and even Jesus could be fiery when circumstances called for a "belly full of fire." Jesus reached into the gene pool of every personality type and found those men and women who could be, with a transformed temperament, Kingdom changers.

William Barclay has said of James, he is "the most tantalizingly vague figure among the twelve." He occupied a leading place among the apostles. He was the first of the apostles to gain the martyr's crown. He was the elder of the two sons of Zebedee. It is strange that he held such a prominent place in history and yet, so little is known about him. There is difficulty in drawing conclusions about James because he never appears apart from John. Perhaps no other apostle suffers more from intervals of silence in his life than James.

As mentioned, he was the son of Zebedee, his mother was Salome, and they made their home in Galilee. Salome had great ambitions for her sons, always wanting the best for them, and at times she was domineering and an outspoken advocate and promoter of her sons. As the testimony of Scripture bears out, it can truly be said that Salome was a brave disciple of Jesus in her own right.

THE CHARACTERISTICS OF JAMES

James was always a person of great courage. After his personal encounter with Jesus Christ, that courage was intermingled with the sweet fragrance of divine grace, which resulted in a former fighter developing a forgiving heart. In Luke 9:52-54, James became infuriated when certain Samaritans refused to accept Jesus' message. He encouraged Jesus to call down judgment on them for their rejection. Yet, in Acts, ever the fiery and faithful disciple, we find James preaching grace and repentance throughout Jerusalem, even while imprisoned for his faith. While no certain facts exist, early Christian tradition says that even at the point of his martyrdom James extended forgiveness to the executioner.

James undoubtedly possessed an acumen for business. By pulling from inference and records of early Jewish historians we can assume that James and his partners gained a certain level of financial affluence. Mark 1:20 indicates that James and his family had the need for employees (servants) to assist in the business, and likely the household as well. His father Zebedee had easy access to the household of the Chief Priest and had the "contract" for supplying fish.

Though in possession of an aggressive personality, there is no record that James ever became jealous of John and Peter. Those two most often appear at the forefront of disciple and apostolic activity, and outside a single incident, James never sought to out muscle Peter and John for more recognition or appreciation in their work alongside Jesus. While the incident involving the request of James and John for seats of honor in the Kingdom elicits a loud gasp from most of us, we can at least commend James for his unflinching faith in the expectation of a coming kingdom. He understood the Old Testament prophecies, he heard the proclamation of John the Baptist, and now Jesus was talking about the Kingdom as though it was just around the next corner. James believed it was! What faith. Though we shrink at his request, James was at least acting on his faith. Such was the zeal that was ever present in his soul. Oh, that the modern church might find a few zealous lovers of Jesus, who like James, live as though the Kingdom is upon us – after all, it is.

As a part of the inner circle, James was among those who, according to Matthew 26:37, were asked by Jesus to accompany Him at little farther into the garden of Gethsemane for a time of prayer. We preachers love to preach about the sleepy disciples who failed to stay awake while just a few steps away a sorrowful Jesus poured out his heart to the Father. Jesus asked about the possibility of the "cup" being avoided. We know that our salvation rested on Jesus' willingness to drink that cup of sorrow. Imagine the shock wave that rippled across Jerusalem when, as recorded in Acts 12:2, James was executed by Herod for continuing his preaching of the gospel. James was the first of the original disciples to drink from the cup of sacrificial death. Eusebius (c.260-c.340) was the first Christian writer to compose an extensive history of the early church. The Bible states that James was killed by the sword (beheaded), and Eusebius tells a story about James' witness to his guards within the prison where he and Peter were held. His account of the event states that one of the guards was converted to Christianity during the trial of James. Faithfulness and zeal until the very end…what more needs to be said?

THE CHALLENGE JAMES ACCEPTED

James was hard at work, mending fishing nets in preparation for the next workday back on the sea. Jesus strolled along the beach, saw the fishermen, and offered this direct invitation, *"Come follow me."* The Bible then tells us that James immediately dropped the nets and followed Jesus. The Bible does not give us the exact time that James had a salvation experience with Jesus, but do not confuse his salvation with this call to service. It appears that Andrew, Peter, John and James had an earlier encounter with Jesus that resulted in their commitment of faith in the claims of Jesus that he was the promised One, who was prophetically declared to be He who would save all people from their sins. The Bible shows us that the fishermen went back to work following that earlier encounter with Jesus. As with many of us, after salvation, there comes a clear, clarion call to ministry. Along that beach James heard that call. For me, though I didn't yet know it, that call was set into motion as I walked away from that military induction center in Montgomery, Alabama. Whatever form of ministry God calls us to, there will be a moment like James had on that beach. Ministry is a calling, be it to pastor, be a missionary, teach children for our church, to write a book, to minister to young adults or pass out gospel tracts on a street corner…whatever God calls us to do for Him, it begins with a definitive call. James was not left to doubt what God was calling him to do… *"Follow me"*… nor did Jesus leave any doubt about the assignment He was giving James, *"I will make you fishers of men."* Every Christian will give an accounting before God (1 Corinthians 3:9-15) for how they carried out their personal, God-given assignment.

Make no mistake; many changes were in store, for James and for all who accept the challenge of serving the Lord. Often, as in the case of James, it may involve a career change. Be sure, for Christians, there are some jobs and professions that are not conducive to living the Christ life. For some the challenge may involve relocating, leaving behind family and friends. May we never forget the admonition of Jesus recorded in Luke 9:62, *"No one who puts his hand to the plow and looks back is fit for the Kingdom of God."*

THE CHANGE JAMES EXPERIENCED

Change is the order of the day when Jesus Christ comes into a life. Things are never the same once Jesus passes by. I previously quoted from a gospel chorus, *I'll Never Be the Same Again.* That chorus also contains these words,

> There are higher heights, there are deeper seas,
>   whatever you need to do, Lord do it in me.
> The glory of the Lord fills my life, and I will never be
>   the same again."

For James there were certain actions would have to change. That nickname, "Boanerges," was given to him for good reason. That nickname means "thunder." Ever met anyone like that? They are capable of "flying off the handle" at the least thing. Such people, and James was one of them, are often loud and bombastic, railing on and on about what may in fact be the smallest of issues. Jesus transformed that tendency in James by taking that trait and immersing it in the Holy Spirit and lighting a fire in the soul of James for the Kingdom of God.

There were many attitudes James harbored that Jesus knew would have to change. Even in the presence of Jesus, the hatred that James carried in his heart for the Samaritans was put on display, and that attitude would have to be changed. James wanted fire to rain down from heaven and destroy these half Jew, half Gentiles who occupied a significant portion of Judea. The Jewish attitude toward Samaritans was made no plainer than in the mere fact that they would avoid even traveling through that section of the nation. When traveling from Judea in the South to Galilee in the North, Jews had rather take a much longer and more dangerous route rather than travel through Samaria. There is no room in the Kingdom of God for such bigotry. James was in Samaria only because John 4:4 says of Jesus, "*He had to pass through Samaria.*" In other words, Jesus had important business to take care of in Samaria. The Bible states that God knows the very thoughts and intents of our minds. There are no secrets we can hide from God.

A forsake all, totally sold-out commitment to Christ will demand that our personal ambitions be put on hold. Chapters nineteen and twenty in Matthew's gospel provide a bit of commentary on matters of ambition. Simon Peter, in Matthew 19:27 basically said, "We gave up everything for you, now, what's in it for us? Then in Matthew 20 is Salome's request that her boys, James and John, be promoted to places of privilege in the Kingdom Jesus was to bring to pass. Wow, such unbridled ambition and greed. Goodness, I am glad we modern day church goers never think or act like those folks. Hah! Of course, we do, don't we? Within the context of those conversations Jesus reminds of the mission He came to implement, and the example for us to follow, "…*the Son of Man came not to be served but to serve…*" Given our human inclinations, a significant shift in attitude and ambition is required of us.

I've said it, perhaps you as well, "He or she died too soon." We mean that this person was good, caring, typically did the right thing – why would they die? Surely, we can say of James, "He died too soon." He was a young man who left behind a lucrative business and in exchange, using the life of Jesus as his model, embarked on a mission to change the world. Are you clinging to anything or anyone that could keep you from being a world changer?

8

NATHANIEL: APOSTLE WITH A FRIEND

W ait! Before you read any further, find a Bible and turn to John's gospel and read the seven verses recorded in 1:45-51. Those seven verses contain the entirely of the Biblical record of the disciple named Nathaniel. We do know that Nathaniel had more than one name by which he was known. If he had lived in our culture today, we perhaps would shorten his name to Nathan, or even Nate. By comparing Scriptures and using the process of elimination and deduction we arrive at the conclusion that Nate, like most of us, had, as we refer to it, a "full" name. I believe that we are therefore, talking about Nathaniel, son of Talmi (Tholmai). Our disciple is Nathaniel Bar Talmai, or Nathaniel Bartholomew.

We would not be wrong to consider Nathaniel a bit of a mystic. As we look closely at the few instances wherein we get a brief glimpse of his activities it can be deduced that he spent a lot of time under a fig tree. There is no conclusive evidence, but it is possible that he was born into a Jewish family – first mentioned in 2 Samuel 13:37 – known as the Tholmaens. If so, Nathaniel was clearly raised in a family that placed a high value on the study of Scripture. Could he have resembled the notion of what "the absent-minded professor" might look like…. hair a bit uncombed, necktie crooked and half-tied, one untied shoelace? He might walk directly past you, never even realizing your presence, living in his own inner world. He may qualify as the most introverted of all the disciples who became an apostle.

Nathaniel may have been a visionary, an aesthetic, with his head in the clouds, yet Jesus saw him as transparent (John 1:47), one He could trust and one who could be depended upon. Jesus saw an apostle in the making.

CONFRONTED BY JESUS

We all need a friend like Philip. After all, it was Philip who upon meeting Jesus, went directly to his friend Nathaniel and then introduced him to Jesus. Philip was convinced that he had met the Messiah, the Promised One of Israel. Note, his first thought was of his friend, who at the time was sitting under a fig tree, which for him was not unusual, for the fig tree had become his place of contemplation and meditation, a place to study and to pray. Philip was straightforward, *"We have found him of whom Moses...and the prophets wrote, Jesus of Nazareth."*

Nathaniel had a friend in Philip, but their conversation suggests that Nathaniel, like many sincere Jews, had a false sense of security. His prejudice bubbled over in his response to his friend, *"Can any good thing come out of Nazareth?"* That was Nathaniel's way of saying that there was no way their deliverer, the Messiah, was going to come from the "wrong side of the tracks." Nathaniel was comfortable in his nationalistic view that the color of his skin, the orthodoxy of his religion, his devout adherence to the Law and its rules, would be enough for him to gain acceptance from the Redeemer once he came to set the Jews free. As stated, it appears that Nathaniel came from a long line of highly religious people who were devotees of the Old Testament. He believed that was enough. Nathaniel felt secure in his beliefs. The walls of his false sense of security had to be broken down, for he was trapped in a system full of prejudices and preconceived ideas that often prove to be among the greatest obstacles to the gospel's redemptive message.

Philip was wise and did not attempt to argue with Nathaniel. Philip's own prejudices and opinions had vanished when he first met Jesus. He knew that an argument would do little to sway the mind of Nathaniel. What great wisdom Philip displayed when he said, *"Come and see."* One could have no greater friend that that one who introduced you to Christ. Philip was indeed such a friend. Who did you last introduce to Jesus?

The first chapter of John is a commentary on personal soul winning. John the Baptist proclaims Jesus as the Lamb of God. Then Andrew and John follow Jesus and spend the day with him and are changed forever. Then Jesus finds Philip, who in turn goes to tell his news about Jesus to Nathanial. Both Philip and Nathaniel were orthodox Jews and had often spoken together on subjects such as God, their nation, and the Messiah. So it was with great passion that upon finding the Messiah that Philip's first thought was of his friend. Who knows, had Nathaniel refused the invitation, then the two friends could have wandered apart, having a theological barrier between them. There can be little doubt that the two friends were brought closer together. Their mutual trust in Christ made this happen. Without fear, hesitation, or apology, Philip told his friend all he had seen and heard, and Nathaniel's interest was aroused enough that he wanted to at least see for himself who this man name Jesus was, and what all the fuss was about.

When Nathaniel met Jesus, all his doubts vanished. He knew that Jesus was no ordinary person. I am not sure about Nathaniel, but I would have been blown away when Jesus said, *"Before Philip called you, when you were under the fig tree, I saw you."* Wow! Nothing is hidden from the Lord and this fact became clear to Nathaniel as he talked with Jesus. Realizing that his heart was an open book to the man from Galilee, he soon surrendered himself to the Galilean. At the moment of that confrontation and revelation of truth, Nathaniel made a life changing, a career changing, a destiny changing declaration, *"You are the son of God, the King of Israel."*

COMMENDED BY JESUS

In Matthew 23: 13-33 Jesus made a strong statement about the overall spiritual condition of Judaism at the time of his earthly ministry. He used terms such as hypocrites, blind guides, blind fools, greedy, self-indulgent, whitewashed grave markers, sons of murderers, vipers and, well…you get the idea. What he saw in his own native religion was a corrupt system that offered little mercy, no grace and failed hope.

Remember, Nathaniel appears to have been very diligent in his allegiance to Judaism, yet when first approached by Jesus there was no finger pointing or accusatory tone in the voice of Jesus. In fact, Jesus was quick to recognize and commend the level of trust that had made its way into the heart of Nathaniel. Nathaniel must have been amazed that the first words of Jesus were not words of condemnation, but instead words of congratulation and encouragement. Nathaniel was a true Israelite, a Jew, not by chance or the accident of birth but in character and disposition and therefore, as a new disciple, there was little to unlearn. Jesus commended Nathaniel for his trust in God.

So, from the first encounter, Jesus saw in Nathaniel a man of honorable character. As an Israelite he was a man who feared God, a man of true simplicity and integrity. Nathaniel had studied the Old Testament and knew of the Messianic promises and the great hope of Israel. As Jesus looked at him, He saw a true son of the covenant. Jesus had an admiration for the ideal character he saw in Nathaniel.

Jesus commended Nathaniel's as one *"in whom there is no guile."* In other words, he was commended for being not only trustworthy, but also transparent. That means Nathaniel did not have a character flawed by dishonesty or duplicity. Frankly, that is a remarkable statement, and we are reminded that in our own present day we find that such a person is a rare commodity. Politics, business, the world of finance and so much of what we see, hear and encounter daily is flawed by continual attempts to conceal the truth and perpetuate a lie. There is no such thing as a half-truth. It is either true or not true.

Nathaniel was one of those rare individuals whose actions in both work and worship were entirely consistent with his inner beliefs. What he professed to be was entirely consistent with who he was. Unlike so many who shared Nathaniel's religious beliefs, there was not an ounce of pretense in his heart.

In him the Lord saw a man of real worth; here was one who was honest in every way. Deceit had never conquered the heart of Nathaniel. There was not a trace of cunning in his nature. Such a man could be trusted, and for that reason he earned the commendation of Jesus.

This characteristic of Nathaniel which was commended by Jesus is not often found in adults. It is more to be found in children, for they tend to be forthright in all their actions and interactions. It is obvious that this characteristic was as rare in Jesus' day as it is in our day.

It is significant that Philip found Nathaniel under the fig tree. That was the place he went to pray and meditate on Scripture. It was there that he opened his soul to God. It is well to note that it was while Nathaniel was in a state of prayer that Jesus revealed Himself to him. The fact that Philip knew where to find Nathaniel would seem to indicate that he regularly prayed. Nathaniel was probably a fisherman by trade, and if his fishing companions ever missed him, they knew they could find him under the fig tree. It was the time and place reserved for prayer that made Nathaniel the guileless Israelite that Jesus wanted in his company of world changers. May we never forget that time praying and reading the Word is an investment with great dividends. Nathaniel found fresh revelation under that fig tree, and even more importantly, he found the real Jesus. Who knows, had Nathaniel missed his private devotional time that day, his life might well have taken a different direction. When it comes to the Bible and prayer we must remain "prayed up" and "read up," for after all, today could be the day our "time is up," and we meet Jesus.

CONFESSED JESUS

Nathaniel's confession was redemptive, *"Rabbi, you are the Son of God! You are the King of Israel."* He had no doubts as to the identity of Jesus. In all of John's gospel we are privy to only seven individual confessions relative to the deity of Jesus Christ. Nathaniel was one of those seven. There was nothing in him to cause him to want to ask, as others had asked, *"Are you the one we are looking for, or should we look for another?"* Nathaniel knew! His confession was that the deity and sovereignty that Christ possessed made him God. None but God could have penetrated the thoughts of his mind or interpreted the desires of his heart as he sat under the fig tree. Suddenly, the identity of Jesus was revealed to him, and his confession bubbled up from his soul. Without any reservation, he assigned to Jesus two of the most grand Messianic titles which expressed the Messianic expectation of that day. Remarkable is the difference between Nathaniel the visionary and Thomas the skeptic. It did not take much of a conversation to convince him that in Jesus Christ, he had met the Messiah.

Nathaniel confessed Jesus first as the Son of God. Most Jews would refuse to believe, but not Nathaniel. He had found the One he had prayed for. While others denied Him, Nathaniel readily confessed Him as the Son of God.

He also confessed Jesus as the King of Israel. Israel had many kings. There were a few good ones, but most of them had been disastrous for the nation. However, in Jesus, Nathaniel knew he had found the true King of Israel. Here was the King of Kings. Now their victory would not just be over some enemy nation, for Jesus will lead his people to victory over the world. Israel had kings who were great diplomats and warriors, but never a king like Jesus. I recognize Jesus as my King, how about you?

CROWNED BY JESUS

Upon Nathaniel's confession, Jesus said, *"greater things that these"* would be revealed to him. In the vernacular of some it was as if

Jesus said, "Nathaniel, you ain't seen nuthin' yet." How encouraging and refreshing that must have been for Nathaniel.

First, Jesus said he would see heaven opened. At the incarnation the heavens opened and God, in Christ, came down. Much like both Simeon and Anna, Nathaniel was hoping and longing for Messiah. His longing was now current reality, and he was standing before the One for whom he had waited. Nathaniel's longing soul had been waiting to see the Lord, and now God incarnate stood before him. Having accepted Jesus as the Messiah, Nathaniel would be given more striking and heavenly revelations.

He was also given the promise that he would see angels ascending and descending. Some have suggested that as Nathaniel sat under the fig tree, he was reading from Genesis 28, about Jacob and the ladder that reached all the way to heaven. Perhaps this was a way of communicating to Nathaniel, as he prepared to leave his father's house, that God would be all to Nathaniel that God had been to the patriarch of old. The angels going up and down the ladder suggest that they are ever at the disposal of Jesus, Nathaniel, and us as well. It is Hebrews 1:14 that tells us that angels are ministering spirits that have been assigned to us.

The ladder suggests that communication with heaven and fellowship with God are possible for all who believe. The ladder represents Christ as Lord, friend, companion, provider, and protector, all in one.

Jesus shared with Nathaniel another title that was most revealing, and that was, Jesus is the "Son of Man." As the Son of God Jesus revealed the good, gracious, and holy nature of God. As the Son of Man, we are assured that he knows all the needs and temptations of we humans. The Lord realizes how feeble we are, how weak if left to our own devices. As Son of Man, Jesus is representative of humanity. Theologically, the only sacrifice that could become the once- and- for- all sacrifice for our sin had to somehow be both God, – for God alone can forgive sin, and that sacrifice must also be human – for it was humanity that had fallen in sin. Only Jesus Christ is capable of being God and man, and thereby meeting those demands.

Nathaniel kept his head in the heavens until the end. His dreams and visions were mighty and noble. He was the lofty apostle who was committed to the King whom he met under a fig tree. There was no looking back, no doubts, no regrets for Nathaniel. There is little more to know for certain. There has long been a verbal tradition that he was flayed to death with knives. While we cannot know, I certainly wish we could know what this thinker, this philosopher, this student of the Word of God, what this faithful disciple saw, in that open door to heaven.

9

JOHN: THE APOSTLE OF FEELING

L ikely, someone, at some time, asked you, "How are you feeling today?" What are they asking you? Are they concerned about your health? Your emotional state? Are they asking for an opinion? Are feelings conscious or unconscious? In the world of psychology, feelings are related to a person's level of emotional awareness. In the business world, on behalf of the then American Express Financial Advisors, I was assigned the role of training financial advisors and their leaders in understanding emotional quotient (EQ), which relates to an individual's so-called emotional intelligence. The notion is that we need to understand and manage our own emotions in a positive way in order to manage stress, communicate effectively, be effective problem solvers, deal with change and effectively manage conflict and crisis. As one might imagine, there are tests given to measure emotional intelligence in a variety of categories. EQ is important to the extent that in almost every possible encounter and exchange we are, either in a one on one situation, or in a group of peers, or as a leader of others, continually engaged in emotional transactions. Teachers, business leaders, salespersons, preachers, volunteer organizations, marriages, and ad infinitum, rise and fall, succeed or fail, on the understanding of the powerful role of our emotions in every human encounter.

John was obviously, at least at times early on, a guy who could have benefited from one of my training sessions on EQ. After all, his nickname, along with his brother James, was "thunder." It must have been a well- earned name, because as you remember, it was Jesus who gave him that nickname.

It is because of this apostle's tremendous capacity to love and be moved with compassion that he is being called "the apostle of feeling." John, along with his brother, was sometimes an explosive man. John was also the youngest of the apostles.

Tradition has somewhat distorted the picture of John. It has been suggested that he was melancholic, mystical, quiet, reserved, and gentle. Artists have painted him as a man with lily white hands and a halo over his head. The very nature of his trade would suggest otherwise. He was a fisherman, certainly a rugged job. The men of the sea were most often men with skin made rough by exposure to the elements, and often their temperaments reflected that rough and tumble lifestyle.

Before his life was transformed by Christ, John often allowed his temperament to dictate his thoughts and responses, which means his decision-making process was often fraught with emotion. He was intolerant, bigoted, and perhaps even a little self-righteous toward those who did not think and believe as he did. Landrum Leavell says John probably knew every four-letter word there was to know. He had a hot heart that often ran high with emotion. You know those guys, right? They typically speak long before they stop to think, and that seldom has a good outcome.

Using LaHaye's terminology, John would react as any choleric would when backed into a corner. Without a flinch or a thought, his feelings would boil over into an outburst.

As we learned earlier, each of us has a dominant component to our personality, which is coupled with a secondary component. For John that secondary aspect of his personality would be labeled by LaHaye as melancholy. As John spent more time with Jesus that element of his personality was drawn out by Jesus, and manifested

itself in John's love, loyalty and unswerving devotion. The obvious
difference is that prior to meeting Jesus, John's choleric
temperament completely dominated him. It was later, after John's
commitment to Jesus that the melancholic tendencies rose to the
top. That's what LaHaye meant by a transformed temperament
(personality). The transforming power of the Holy Spirit can take a
cussing, brawling sailor like John, and transform him into the writer
of the gospel of John, three letters and the book of Revelation.
Enemies of the gospel tried to kill John many times but failed. John
kept on loving (he became known as the apostle of love), witnessing
and writing, outliving every other early follower of Jesus. The
apostle Paul, in Romans 12 said, *"be transformed by the renewing of your
mind."* The mind is the seat of our emotions and intelligence, and to
be our most effective as a disciple of Jesus, we must continually
allow the transformation agent of the Godhead (the Holy Spirit) to
invade and control our thought world, *"taking captive every thought."*

John was the son of Zebedee and the brother of James, and the
two of them were in business with Peter and Andrew. A close
connection between Peter and John extended beyond business. They
fished together, and in Mark 1:29 John went to Peter's house for the
services of the Sabbath. It was Peter and John who were sent to
prepare the Passover feast during the final week of Jesus life, and
early in Acts they were preaching partners and were predominant in
the early success of the church.

John was indeed an apostle of feeling. H.S. Vigeveno in *Thirteen
Men Who Changed the World,* titles the chapter on John, "From
Temper to Tenderness." He says, "If you want theology read Paul,
if you want ethics read James. But if you want to know about love,
if you want the heart of Christianity, you must read John."

John was one of the members of the inner circle of Jesus,
composed of Peter, James, John, and at times Andrew. They were
with the Lord on special and significant occasions. Of the four, John
was likely closer to Jesus than any of the others. If this was true of
the four, then it is certainly true of the twelve. What an enviable
position, to walk in such close fellowship with Jesus. John was truly
the apostle of love. Jesus took him as a rough, angry man of the sea,

and transformed him into a compassionate winner of souls and writer of the good news.

A MAN OF HONOR

John was indeed a man of honor. A glance at the background of John reveals why he could be counted as a man of honor.

He was a man of honor first because of his parents. John was the son of Zebedee and Salome. Zebedee appears to have been a man of means and a very influential man among the Jews. It appears that Zebedee's business was a supplier for the household of the High Priest, which created continual access to the High Priest. A look at Scripture indicates that his fishing business was not a small operation at all. When Jesus came and called John from the boat of his father, the Bible says they left him in the boats with "the hired servants." This surely pointed to a measure of wealth and to a degree of success in the business. Their fishing business was large enough to demand hired help to man the boats and haul in the catch.

As already indicated, his father Zebedee was known in the house of the high priest. John 18:15, in relating the account of Jesus before the high priest, tells of another disciple who was present. That other disciple had to be John. He, like his father, was known in the house of the high priest. This explains why he had no difficulty in gaining entrance to the meeting. Perhaps he had been there many times before with his father. His face was recognized by the servants and guards of the house, thus giving him complete access to the premises.

The mother of John was a wonderful woman by the name Salome. Salome is considered to have been a believer, and in fact, Salome was probably the aunt of Jesus. At the cross of Jesus there were certain women who stood there intently aware of all that was happening that day. Mark records these women as Mary Magdalene, Mary the mother of James the Less and of Joses, and Salome. John's list looks like this: Jesus' mother, his mother's sister, Mary the wife of Cleophas, and Mary Magdalene. Matthew's gospel lists them as Mary Magdalene, Mary the mother of James and Joses, and the mother of Zebedee's children. Mary the mother of James and Joses and Mary the wife of Cleophas are the same person. That being so, the remaining person is called Salome, the sister of Jesus' mother and the mother of Zebedee's children. That would then make the two brothers, James and John, cousins of Jesus.

What a blessing it was for John to have such fine parents. He had the advantage of a God-fearing home. Perhaps his mother spent many sleepless nights, prior to his conversion, wondering where he was and what trouble he might invite. No doubt she prayed for John that God would take over his life and calm him down and control his spirit. She would have been no different than any mother who loved and prayed for her son.

John was also a man of honor because of his profession. The trade of fisherman was a very honorable business. It was a business exposed to all kinds of weather elements, and a trade that required taking many risks. These experiences could have shaped John into a stern, disciplined man. John was a man with hands hardened by the toil of the sea and skin bronzed by the glaring sun. The profession had made him strong and daring, and he was probably never frightened by ordinary circumstances. It must have been that sense of daring and adventure that sent John, on the night of Jesus' arrest, into the house of Caiaphas. Truthfully, Jesus seems to have called him as much for his strength as his tenderness.

It is so important that one's profession be that which would become a Christian. Affiliation in the wrong business practices could destroy a witness for Christ. John was an honorable man; he worked hard, and must have been an honest businessman, enabling him and his family to have a firmly established business.

A third reason to consider John as a man of honor is because of his designated place in religion. John was first a disciple of John the Baptist. His time spent in the desert wilderness served as spiritual preparation, a training ground for the calling he would receive from Jesus. There is no indication as to how long John attended those meetings with the Baptist, but the day came when he heard the

Baptist say, *"Look, the Lamb of God."* John never forgot that day. He was accustomed to going to the synagogue, and therefore familiar with Old Testament Scriptures which spoke of the Messiah as the Lamb of God. Beginning that day, from that first moment, John was captivated, and he was on his way to becoming a fisher of men.

John was that other disciple who, with Andrew, like little puppies, followed Jesus home one day. In modesty he concealed his own name. There are four possible stages in the spiritual development of John. The first of these is in John 1:35, 40 and may very well be the point of conversion and becoming a disciple of the Baptist. Then there is that moment recorded in John 1:40 when John left and followed Jesus. Matthew 4:21,22 shows John as a disciple being taught by the Jesus himself. The final stage of development came when John is referred to as an apostle. He was sent, that is what the word apostle means – somewhat like a missionary - by the Lord into ready fields that awaited harvesting. John was among the first chosen for discipleship. He was a man of faith and feeling and fervor, and his place in the Kingdom work of Christ on earth is memorialized in heaven.

A fourth thing that made John a man of honor was his position in Christ. The Bible proclaims him as the "disciple whom Jesus loved." John was an intolerant man who found it easier to call fire down from heaven than to be meek under pressure. So, there were many lessons of humility to be learned, and his teacher was the Master himself. John was certain of his position in Christ. He was saved (redeemed and set free), sanctified (cleaned up) set apart for service (called by Jesus) and sealed (secured a place with God forever), all of which is borne out by the faithful life he lived for Christ.

John was a man who was loyal to Christ in every way. Evidence of his unending love and loyalty to Christ is seen in an incident in Mark 9:38. This is one of the few times in the Bible when James is not mentioned alongside John. John had seen a man casting out devils in the name of Jesus. The man was not actually a member of their company of disciples. John went to the man and prohibited him from performing any ministry. Jesus gently told him to let the man be, explaining that anyone who was not against them was for them.

In the New Testament, the beloved disciple is seen as he leaned on Jesus' breast (John 13:21-25). The practice of the day was for the people at a feast to recline on low couches with their feet stretched out behind them. It was also the custom in a Jewish home for the youngest child to occupy a chair next to the father of the house during the Passover meal. That is a practice still honored in Jewish homes to this day. John was the youngest of the disciples and would have been near Jesus on the evening of that "last supper" in the upper room. It was to the care of the beloved disciple that Jesus entrusted Mary his mother. It was the beloved disciple who arrived first at the tomb on Easter morning. The beloved disciple was at the lakeside when Jesus appeared to his men. He was loved by the Lord, and John repaid that love with both love and world-changing faith. John's commitment was the "real deal." At age ninety his fellow apostles and his family were all gone. Yet, there he is, to the very end, still filled with the Holy Spirit, still celebrating the Lord's Day, still seeing visions and hearing from God. What a life, what a victor!

A HERALD OF LOVE

John was a herald of the good news in every way, in every place he traveled. Everything that he did spoke of his love for Christ. Love became the theme of all that John ever said or did. No other writer, religious or secular, has ever declared love in the manner of John. What John knew about love could have been learned only from the Lover of mankind Himself. More than eighty times John speaks of love in his writings. He saw love not as a sentiment, but as a principle and a life-changing virtue. Love as John understood it could be classified in this manner:

1. God is One of Love. John 5:42, 15:10
2. God loved His Son. John 10:17, 15:9, 17:23,24,26
3. God loved the disciple. John 16:27, 17:23
4. God loves all men. John 3:16

5. God is loved by Christ. John 14:31
6. Christ loved the disciples in general. John 13:1-34; 14:21, 15:9,10
7. Christ loved individuals. John 11:5, 36; 13:23
8. Christ expected all men to love Him and God. John 8:42; 14:23
9. Christ taught that we should love one another. John 13:34,35; 15:12,13
10. Christ emphasized that love is the sum and substance of the Law, and that the Law can be truly kept as one loves God and others. Exodus 20:1-17; Matthew 22:36-40

The commandment of the Lord was to love God and then to love our neighbor. John exemplified the fulfilled of that commandment as well as any human could ever do so.

John was a herald of Christ through his bold witness. The word "witness" is found in John's writings thirty times. Words which refer to the same thing such as "record" is used thirteen times and "testify" or "testimony" twenty-five times. He begins by saying that John the Baptist was a witness of Christ as the light and that men were brought to believe because of that witness. John became a greater witness himself, for he walked personally with Jesus. He presents the message of Jesus as fact. He sets forth most reliable evidence of the fact:

1. The witness of the Baptist. John 5:32,33
2. The witness of the Scripture. John 5:39
3. The witness of the Father. John 5:37
4. The witness of Christ Himself. John 8:14
5. The witness of Christ's miracles. John 5:36
6. The witness of the Holy Spirit. John 15:26
7. The witness of the disciples. John 15:27

John was a man to whom the Lord revealed himself in a mighty and magnificent way. He was the first to see the reality of the resurrection (an empty tomb), and as an accurate witness he described what he saw in detail, even to the position of the clothing left behind. He was the first to discern the Lord's appearance on the lakeside and he described all that took place. The Revelation of John comes in the form of an apocalyptic prophecy. Throughout the Revelation Christ is presented as the "Faithful Witness."

Before John's witness to the world could include the great truths of God, it was necessary for him to experience God's glory in its fullness. John was a witness to the glory of Jesus Christ for over seventy years. No matter the circumstances, his love for Jesus remained passionate and his eyewitness account of the ministry of Jesus is unparalleled in Scripture.

The style of John is unique in many respects. John makes his sentences so that they can stand alone. Bible scholars have said that John's style is "contemplative, not controversial; calm, not militant; simple, yet profound; direct rather than oblique; transparent, yet deep; spiritual rather than historical."

John always elevates Jesus to a position of supremacy in all his writings. As he wrote of the marvelous glory of Christ, he did so in a simple, yet profound way. Guided and filled with the Holy Spirit, his writings carry us beyond the earthly realm and allow us to see, to hear and to experience that which remains a mystery to unsaved, and even to believers who never develop an intimate relationship with Christ.

John, in his modest fashion, did not put his name anywhere in his gospel. It has been called the "gospel of conversations" since it relates to the individuals that had an interview with Jesus Christ. Altogether there were twenty-four conversations held with seventeen people in John's gospel. These conversations were often brief discourses and sometimes they were teaching that came as a prelude or postscript to a miracle. The purpose of the gospel is stated in John 20:31, "...*these are written so that you may believe that Jesus is the Christ, the Son of God, and that by believing you may have life in his name.*" John was ever the evangelist. Whether preaching, writing, teaching or praying, John's heart was always focused on that next person who needed to know about Jesus. Personal evangelism, if it even exists in the context of the modern church, has been relegated to the job description of the professional staff. We would do well to heed Proverbs 11:30, *"…whoever captures souls is wise."* John, as a student of the Bible, would have read that text more than a few times. The KJV says, *"He that is wise winneth souls."* The work of soul winning – capturing souls – is not the work of professionals. It is the calling and assignment of every Christian, and almost every day, each us will have at least one opportunity to have a gospel conversation with another person. In many of those instances only eternity will disclose the eventual outcome. Other opportunities will result in us being allowed to celebrate the outcome. The point is this, like John, we must grab each of those opportunities and do what John did… show them Jesus. John's relentless desire was to lead others to a belief in the historical Christ, and to a saving belief in the person of Christ.

Certain words just seem to jump from the pages within the gospel of John, and those words reveal so much about the very character of John's writing. The word light appears twenty-three times; life, fifty-two times; love, seven times; truth, twenty-five times; true, five times; witness, forty-seven times; believe, ninety-eight times; world, seventy-eight times; sign, seventeen times. Those words, as well as our words, can and should reveal our love for Jesus.

The exalted theme of the first epistle (letter) of John is love. It is addresses one of the early problems of the church; that of some denying the humanity of Christ.

John writes about the love of God in redemption and presents it as a motive for holiness and mutual love. He presents many tests for the sincerity of our profession as a Christian.

The second and third letters appear to be written by John as he had grown older and now there is some issue or issues that need to be addressed, and who better to do that than an Elder? These two letters comprise the shortest books in the New Testament. The immediate problem that is addressed in both letters is related to how the local church is to receive traveling preachers. At issue is such matters as trust (how do we know who is a false teacher), pay (do they get paid, and how much), and length of stay (what if they stay too long). It is clear from John's teachings that there was always agreement among local Christians as to how they would treat and react to these preachers, even those deemed not to be true preachers of the gospel. These two letters serve as a reminder that in every generation the Christian churches will have problems and disagreements. John's letters serve to remind us that we must lovingly and scripturally deal with those issues and bring them to a point of resolution. Left undone in the church, little things become big things and the ensuing discord is the enemy of the church.

The final book from John's pen is the last book in the Bible. His name is not mentioned in his gospel or the any of the letters, but his name appears five times in Revelation. The visions contained in Revelation were given by Christ to His much-loved apostle. Those visions came to John while exiled on the Isle of Patmos, a desolate place used by the Romans as a place to put prisoners in isolation. The writings from Patmos were not published until some period following John's death.

All the writings of John came from the pen of a man who was standing at the foot of the cross when Jesus gave His life on Calvary. His writings show that John was inspired to write about some significant matters that either escaped the notice of the other gospel writers, or for whatever reason were passed over.

John was also a herald of Christ through his work. In other words, John's life proved to be a living testimony of his faith in Christ. It is one thing to stand and verbally testify as to how much we love Jesus. It is quite another thing for the character and actions of our life to speak louder than our words. The New Testament reveals in John, one who from that first day when he and Andrew followed Jesus home, right up until John, then an old man, died on a desolate island. He never lost his passion, and he never stopped telling the story.

A HERO OF THE FAITH

John was a man of valor and courage. Through every experience he became stronger in his faith and commitment.

John became a prisoner of Nero. One might wonder why a

great emperor would be afraid of a ninety-year-old converted Jewish man. Persecution had ceased somewhat until the new Emperor Domitian ascending to the throne. From that day forward a new wave of persecution broke out against the church. John was preaching in Asia Minor when the emperor learned of his Christian activity. An edict was sent out saying that John was to be seized and sent to Patmos, banished and left to die.

Patmos was surrounded by the sea which made escape impossible. But while on that island, John was caught up into the third heaven and heard the message *"there shall be no more sea."* While that may seem a strange thing to write, when put into the context of Jewish thinking, it is not at all strange. To most Jews the sea was a dark, often turbulent place. It was a place that swallowed up entire ships, along with cargo and all the people on board the ship. It was a dangerous and fearful place and was to to be avoided if possible. So here on Patmos, surrounded by all the dark, often turbulent water, was John. Culturally, the absence of such a place was a good thing. So yes, John is looking toward that time when all fears are gone, work is done, and we find perfect rest in the place Jesus promised he was preparing for us.

From John comes an example for all to follow. We would do well to emulate the life of John. The length and the influence of his witness was remarkable, yet the greatest thing about his entire life and testimony is what the Lord did for John. May we never forget that what Christ did for John He stands ready to do for every believer. The Savior John knew was the One he had seen, and heard, and experienced on a human level. John learned to walk in the light and love that was at the core of Jesus, for after all, He was God. John's desire was to become like Him. This son of thunder was transformed into the apostle of love, who learned that expressing his feelings had nothing to do with his masculinity. He was an erupting volcano of human emotion, turned into a free-flowing fountain of affection. May each of us experience such a transformation.

10

PHILIP: THE APOSTLE WHO WAS FOUND

The twelve disciples who became the original twelve apostles all had a strong Jewish heritage, yet Philip is a Greek name. It was not uncommon during that early period of time for individuals, including Jews, to have both a Greek name and a culturally based name. The Greek military dominance preceding the Roman period had left a cultural impact on many societies, and the Jewish society was no exception. Perhaps the greatest gift left behind by the Greeks was the gift of language. My favorite Christmas Scripture is found in Galatians 4:4, *"But when the fullness of time had come, God sent forth his Son, born of a woman, born under the law, to redeem those who were under the law, so that we might receive adoption as sons."* Jesus' birth was right on time. God had orchestrated all things relative to the timing of Jesus' birth, including the great gift of language from the Greeks. Thus, when it came time for the disciples to fulfill Acts 1: 8, there was a common language available to them in facilitating the spread of the gospel. The Greek language was spoken most places, including Israel, so, it is understandable that Philip had a Greek name. Within Israel the "Hellenist" Jews preferred to speak the Greek language, as well as adopting many aspects of Greek culture and customs. In Acts 6:1 there arose a controversy in the Jerusalem church, and it involved treatment of the Hellenistic Jews. It is likely Philip had a Jewish name to accompany his Greek name, however, the Bible is silent on that fact.

A point of clarification in this introduction to Philip's ministry will enable us to ensure that we fully understand who disciple Philip is, and that he is not confused with deacon Philip. In Acts 6:5 the early Jerusalem church was electing the first deacons, and Philip was among those seven men who were elected deacons. Philip the deacon, according to the testimony of Acts 6 was a man with an honorable reputation, a man of faith, full of the Holy Spirit and given to making wise decisions. In Acts 8 we find a man named Philip engaged in ministry as a traveling preacher – an evangelist. The Philip in Acts 8 and Acts 6 is the same person. Deacon Philip became Evangelist Philip, not Apostle Philip. This Deacon Philip, and our Apostle Philip in John 12, are two different individuals. I find it interesting that the Bible tells us more about Deacon Philip than about Apostle Philip.

HIS TESTIMONY

Only John's gospel tells us anything about Philip the apostle. John gives us three brief glimpses of Philip, and from those we are left to draw inferences about his character and his personality. It seems that he was reserved, perhaps even shy. From John we can draw the conclusion that Philip was quick with numbers. If he were around today his aptitude with math and numbers might push him toward a career in accounting. His temperament would likely lean toward one who would say, "just show me the facts." Shy? Perhaps. Calculating? Probably. One thing is clear, Philip was a seeker who was found – and upon being found Philip did what we all should do – he went to find a friend (Nathaniel) that he might tell him about Jesus.

I think it significant that Philip was found by Jesus. I know, you're thinking, so what, others were also found by Jesus. However, in terms of discipleship, Philip was the first person to be called by Jesus, the first to hear the words, *"come follow me."* Sure, by the time Philip became a disciple there were others who had already begun a relationship with Jesus. Peter, James, John and Andrew were already well acquainted with Jesus and had managed to spend personal time with him. Yet, In John 1:42-43 the Bible says, *"The next day Jesus decided to go to Galilee. He found Philip and said to him, 'Follow me.'"*

I think that Philip was not only found by Jesus, I also think he was likely nurtured in his faith by friends. Goodness, every person new in their faith needs a mentor, a coach, someone to teach them the basics. Because Philip was from Bethsaida one might say that he was from "the wrong side of the tracks." In Matthew 20: 20-24 Jesus denounces three cities for their wickedness and their lack of remorse and repentance for their lifestyle and their beliefs. Philips's hometown, Bethsaida was one of those three cities. Tough place for one wanting to follow Jesus, don't you agree? Well, it so happens that Philip had two friends from Bethsaida – Andrew and Peter – who had recently discovered Jesus for themselves. Philip was not alone in his new faith. He had friends who shared his faith. I feel confident that the three had attended the same synagogue and were to some degree friends, before now sharing faith in Christ. Being a disciple is about learning and being taught. Discipleship, the calling of every Christian, is helping others learn more about Jesus and His claims on our lives. I am always asking myself who it is that I have discipled lately. May we never forget that the commission to make disciples, is the commission that Jesus has put before us, and may we never fail to seek out opportunities to walk alongside those new in their faith, for that is the very definition of discipleship.

In each case where Philip is mentioned in Scripture, he had to be sought out. When he was called, Jesus sought him. At the feeding of the five thousand, Jesus sought him. When the Greeks sought Jesus, Philip turned them over to Andrew. It appears that Philip was shy and retiring and yet he served the Lord faithfully, not with propaganda but performance. He was analytical and quick with figures but slow to arrive at final decisions. Philip seemed to have the analytical abilities of the melancholic and the practicality of the phlegmatic. Those characteristics could have led him to postpone making decisions, based on the notion that more data, more information might be available. Such individuals often have a fear of making a mistake, often leading to the mistake of not taking action even when in possession of adequate information.

HIS TRANSFORMATION

Philip was a practical man, a pragmatist, who needed certain proof before he would believe anything. He believed in those things he could feel or touch or see. He was what some refer to as a levelheaded man. While Philip was open and ready to hear anyone and their ideas, that, however, was never going to mean he would accept what he heard at face value.

Philip's introduction to Jesus came from no individual. Others had been directed to Jesus by John the Baptist, but not Philip; he was sought and found by Christ himself. He has the distinction of being the first to, upon meeting Jesus, immediately follow Jesus. Andrew, John, and Peter had found Jesus but had returned to their boats. Not Philip. When he met Christ he believed, and he followed right then.

John's gospel has recorded an interesting order of seeking and finding. Andrew found the Messiah and then went and found Simon. Later Philip found Nathaniel. Throughout the Bible there seems to be a law of seeking and finding. In fact, the promise of the Lord is, *"he that seeks, finds."* This principle can be applied to soul winning as well as salvation. If one is faithfully seeking to bring others to Christ, then God is going to bless with a harvest of souls. Thousands have never known the Lord and never will unless someone seeks them and finds them for Jesus.

Philip had friends who helped him grow spiritually. Andrew and Peter were close friends of Philip, and Andrew seems to have been Philip's father in the faith. He turned to Andrew when difficulties arose. Those two hometown friends were a tremendous blessing to Philip.

One of the most important things about Philip is that he put his faith to work. Once he had been found by Jesus, he went out and began to find others. He was a new convert who quickly became an evangelist. He had been saved and then he served with relentless passion.

The first individual that Philip went to find was Nathaniel. Some have suggested that Nathaniel was the brother of Philip while others say he was a good friend. Regardless of their relationship, Nathaniel was the closest person to Philip, and he went to tell him about Jesus. What a testimony! Family or friends, why would we not tell them? Is it fear? Do we somehow feel embarrassed? Do we fear rejection? Whatever our hesitation, our lack of action, may we model Philip and others like him, who relentlessly seemed to be looking for the next person to tell about Jesus.

We have all known individuals like Philip, who never shy from introducing anyone, anywhere, anytime to Jesus. For many years I had the privilege of watching R.A. Sharp, a layperson in our church, who had an unparalleled passion for reaching the unconverted for Christ. In the everyday language of the church, we refer to that as soulwinning. R.A. was never bashful when it came time to bring up the subject of an individual's personal relationship with Christ. He was always ready to talk about Jesus. No matter the person, no matter the circumstances, no matter the location – R.A. knew he was under a divine mandate to keep telling the gospel story of "ruin to redemption." Many a person is, or will be, in heaven because R.A., like Philip, was never shy about introducing a person to Jesus.

Philip eagerly told Nathaniel that they had found him of whom Moses and the prophets spoke. Nathaniel was skeptical, but Philip did not argue; he simply said, "come and see." Two things occur to me regarding Philip. First, he had a missionary instinct. He was determined to share Christ. Furthermore, he had the right approach. He did not allow himself to be drawn into an argument. We should always pray for God to give us opportunities to share our story and our faith with others, but we should also pray for wisdom in making the most of that opportunity. A winsome spirit is far more likely to be welcomed than an argumentative confrontation. We might win the debate, but all too often we close the door on the opportunity to eventually influence that person for Christ. We must learn to confront without being confrontational. Jesus said, *"He that seeketh, findeth…"* John's gospel make it clear how that statement is applicable in gospel relationships…Andrew found Jesus, then he found his brother Peter. Philip was found by Jesus, and Philip then found Nathaniel. Current reports and surveys tell us that America is moving away from church and away from God. As American society becomes more secularized and political socialism grows in popularity, we are reminded that thousands upon thousands are on outside looking in relative to the Kingdom of God. Unless those like Philip, and my friend R.A. Sharp step up, we will continue to lose generations who may never know Jesus in a personal way. When it comes to soulwinning, the law of seeking and finding has not been shelved.

HIS TESTING

Chapter six in John's gospel opens with a worried Philip. More than five thousand people had followed Jesus out into the countryside to get a glimpse of him and to listen to his teaching. Given Philip's personality I have little doubt that he was thinking about a particular issue long before Jesus put a question before him. Perhaps Philip's assignment among the disciples was that of logistical manager. Why else would Jesus expect Philip to answer his question. And what was that question? *"Where are we to buy bread, so that these people may eat?"* The Bible clearly states that Jesus presented the question as a test for Philip. Jesus already knew the answer. Philip had already asked that question in his mind…how can we feed this many hungry people? Obviously, Philip knew a lot about math and accounting, but he did not know enough about miracles and how God's supply chain works.

Philip had calculated what it would take to feed such a crowd. In the back of his mind, he knew that a year's pay would not be enough to buy enough food for the large crowd. One denarius normally bought twelve wheat or thirty-six barley loaves, which were about an inch and a half thick.

One might wonder why Philip was singled out by the Lord. Jesus certainly did not turn to Philip in need of information as to how the need would be met. The question was an educational one. The circumstance was a trial of Philip's faith in the power of Christ. The common purse of the apostles contained only two hundred pennies, a far cry from what was needed.

Philip's response came from a business mind rather than a believing heart. He was thinking in material terms what it would cost to feed the multitude. The intention of Jesus was to test Philip's faith and deepen his grasp of the divine mission they were engaged in every day.

Philip's response was not much different than the response of many of us when confronted with circumstances that demand action and answers. We often seek a way in which we can personally work out the problem. I have made those same calculations, many times, and arrived at a similar conclusion…this can't be done! Of course, it can't – not until we bring the Lord into the equation and then turn in simple faith to Jesus – forgetting my own ill-conceived plans and replacing them with a divine plan. This is a human weakness found in many. Philip needed to know that with Christ all things are possible, and I am still trying to learn that lesson each day.

The outcome, when Jesus interjected himself into the quandary, was miraculous. Philip saw another demonstration of the power of Christ. He had failed to account for the divine power of Jesus, but in the presence of all in attendance, Jesus took the lunch basket of one little boy and produced a meal that was satisfying to everyone. As always in the case of Christ, there was enough and to spare.

THE TRUTH HE LEARNED

In John 14:8 we discover Philip, along with the other disciples, gathered in the upper room prior to the arrest and eventual crucifixion of Jesus. Jesus was encouraging them regarding his soon departure. He explained that even though he was going to be absent for a time, he would come back for them. During that conversation, in reply to a question from Thomas, Jesus remarked that *"if you had known me, you would have known my Father also."* At that statement Philip spoke and said, *"Lord, show us the Father, and it is enough for us."* The response of Jesus was, as recorded in the Message Bible, *"You've been with me all this time, Philip, and you still don't understand?"* I think every pastor and every teacher must have thought, if not said, those very words. I have arrived at the 54th anniversary of my call into ministry. I have now been teaching the Bible at the same church for 34 years, and some Sundays I leave church shaking my head – "You still don't get it." Philip had failed to grasp what Jesus had just said to Thomas. Philip's mind had gone racing down a rabbit hole and thought only of physically seeing the Father. He missed out on the lesson – in Christ we have a spiritual connection that allows us to experience God, even in our everyday, sometimes mundane, experiences. God is ever present. Had Philip lived and walked side by side with Jesus for three years and yet did not yet understand who he was? My ministry experience has taught me that Philip's thoughts and words are not unique. The response of Jesus serves to remind us that knowing is not conditioned upon seeing. I observe Christians chasing the next "big" experience with God. They hop from conference to conference, church to church, as if they can just somehow see the next exciting move of God, they will then get the confirmation of "it," whatever "it" is. Like Philip, they have not grasped the spiritual reality that as Christians we are allowed to continually dwell in the presence of Almighty God, and to walk in His Spirit, and to abide (live) in Christ. The complete revelation of God stood directly before Philip, yet he asked to see more. Philip did not get it. Do you?

11

THADDAEUS: APOSTLE OF FAITH

S omeone once referred to Thaddaeus as one of the "lesser
lights" among the early disciples. I beg to disagree with such an
assessment. First, in God's greater Kingdom there are no lesser
lights. All we who are saved by grace have equal standing with God.
Yes, it is true that certain individuals create for themselves a more
visible reputation than others, but may we never forget that the
apostle Paul reminds us in his first letter to the Corinthian church
that God's assessment of such matters as wisdom and nobility and
ability are far different than man's assessment.

Thaddaeus was not likely a highly visible force in the life of the
early church, perhaps like James "the Less," he worked unnoticed in
the background most of the time. This does not mean that he was
any less important than the others, only that he was quiet and
retiring. Thaddaeus probably asked Jesus the last question any
apostle asked him before Gethsemane. The question of Thaddaeus
was, "How is it you will reveal yourself to us and not to the world?"
The response of Jesus was quite telling in that Jesus basically offered
a two-part response. First, He reminded the disciples that love for
Jesus is revealed by living out the Word of God. "*If anyone loves me, he
will keep my word…*" The heart of Jesus' answer to the question of

Thaddaeus came in these words, *"The Holy Spirit...will teach you all things and bring to remembrance all that I have said to you."* So, how is that to this very day, although Jesus is not visibly present to any of us, we continue to get fresh revelation from Jesus? The answer lies in the two things Jesus said to the disciples, that is we maintain our relationship with our teacher, the Holy Spirit, and we stay committed to the Word of God. If we do that, we will continue to have both revelation from, and a relationship with, Jesus Christ.

Although we don't know much about him, we can rest assured that Thaddaeus had a defining moment when he met Christ. That defining moment was followed by a decisive moment when he heard Jesus say, "follow me." Clearly, Thaddaeus decided to follow Jesus. Jesus said in John 12:26, *"Whoever serves me must follow me."* Every encounter with Jesus Christ demands a decision and a response. An unknown writer penned these words which became a well used hymn:

> *I have decided to follow Jesus...*
> *The world behind me, the cross before me...*
> *Tho' none go with me, I still will follow...*

> *Will you decide now to follow Jesus?*

Thaddaeus responded in the affirmative to the call of Jesus. Early writers referred to him as the "steadfast" apostle. What a compliment! Many begin the journey with Jesus, but something happens along the way and the once burning fire for Christ becomes but warm embers or cold ashes. Not Thaddaeus; there was no turning back.

HIS DISTINCTION

His name in Aramaic means bold and courageous. If his name truly depicts his character, then he must have been a very bold fellow. Given a few facts and assumptions we can make about his life, it is likely he belongs to the Sanguine category (personality), even though much of his time was spent living and working in the background. In many ways he represents those persons every pastor wishes he had more of in the congregation. Someone with a boldness for Jesus. Someone who works and works without demanding credit and recognition. Someone who is always there, no matter the task.

While not unique to Thaddaeus, one of the distinctive things about him was that he was a man with multiple names. The name Thaddaeus, which means devoted, is the Greek derivative of a Jewish name. A Jewish writer, Alfred Edersheim, says that his name means praise. Both Matthew (chapter 10) and Mark (chapter 3) refer to him as Thaddaeus. He is also referred to in the Bible (Luke 6:16; John 14:22; Acts 1:13) as Judas – "not Iscariot." Judas is a Hebrew name derived from the word Judah. The name Judah means "Jehovah leads." Judas became a very popular name among Jews following the Maccabean period in Jewish history. Judas Maccabees was a priest who led the Maccabean revolt that led to the removal of statues of Greek gods and goddesses that had been erected in Jewish places of worship in the period of 167-160 BC. His most notable victory resulted in driving out the defilers of the Temple of Jerusalem on December 14, 164 BC. Hanukkah celebrates the purification of that Temple. Some legends give him the nickname, "the hammer." Given Judas' well documented exploits, one can understand why many parents chose to name their sons Judas. It remained a treasured and revered name until the treasonous actions of Judas Iscariot. Matthew's gospel (chapter 10) records yet another name attributed to Thaddaeus, and that name is Labbaeus, which means "heart child." Writer Herbert Lockyer states that Judas was his primary name, with other names added by various apostles.

It bears pointing out that another point of distinction for Thaddaeus is the great likelihood that he harbored militaristic ambitions. While one of his names may have meant tender hearted, his closest friends appear to have been Zealots. As we have already discussed in previous chapters, the Zealots were Jews who detested Roman rule over the Jews, and they were willing to take aggressive action in the form of guerrilla warfare in the back streets and alleys of the cities. The Zealots also had a strong religious belief relative to

Messiah, and that was that He would come as a military leader who would destroy all the enemies of the Jews. Many believe that at least four Zealots were called by Jesus as early disciples. (Judas Iscariot, Simon the Cananite, Thaddaeus and James, the son of Alphaeus.)

We are unable to identify the maternal lineage of Thaddaeus, but we do know that his father's name was James. Like the name Judas, James was another often-used name of the time period. Scriptural information is not adequate to make any further assumptions about the family of Thaddaeus. Jerome called him "Trinomius," which means a man with three names.

HIS DISCIPLESHIP

There are several things that mark Thaddaeus as a true disciple. One of those things is the fact that he was hungry to learn all he could about Jesus. A disciple is a learner and Thaddaeus had a desire to learn all that he could from, and about, Jesus. From John 14:22 it is apparent that he had a curiosity about spiritual matters and was not ashamed to ask questions. Thaddaeus knew that he needed to be taught and he was willing to explore all the possibilities in order to be spiritually informed. The questions which Thaddaeus asked shows his desire, a hunger for spiritual understanding, in order that he might have solid basis for the mission that was soon to be thrust upon him.

True disciples not only experience and express a spiritual hunger to more fully know and understand Kingdom principals, but true disciples always exhibit honesty and humility when approaching Jesus. In John 6:60-70 is a moment when Jesus more clearly defined discipleship, and he did as we sometimes say, "drew a line in the sand," and waited to see who would cross the line. Many (thousands) had come out to hear Jesus teach and to see his miracles. One response to his teaching and preaching is found in verse sixty, *"this is too hard, we can't listen anymore."* Wow! Verse sixty-six then states, *"After this many of his disciples turned back and no longer walked with him."* Double wow! Every pastor can relate to that experience. Most teachers of church Bible classes can relate as well. Too hard...too long…too much required…too this, too that….wow! Jesus then turned to the twelve and looked them square in the eyes and asked, *"Do you want to go away as well?"* Ouch! In other words, Jesus was wondering out loud if anyone was willing to truly follow him. Luke chapter nine is a comprehensive course, taught by Jesus, on the course and cost of discipleship. Many line up and say, "I'm ready Jesus, but first…." In Luke 9:62 (MSB) Jesus said this, *"No procrastination. No backwards looks. You can't put God's Kingdom off until tomorrow. Seize the day."* You might as well be honest with Jesus and his invitation to *"come, follow me."* In John 6 as Jesus spoke, not to the large crowd, but to the twelve when he said, *"Did I not choose you, the twelve? But one of you is a devil."* Jesus knew! It is not about what our lips say, it's what our heart says about Jesus that matters. Thaddaeus was forthright and honest when he accepted the invitation of Jesus to follow, and there was no turning back.

HIS DARK PAST

By dark past, I am not making a reference to anything nefarious about his past life. As said, he appears to have been at least philosophically in agreement with the Zealots, but we have no record of an unsavory lifestyle. By dark I simply mean that neither the Bible nor historical records bring illumination to his history. History is silent about Thaddaeus, yet there are lessons to be learned from his obscurity.

First, though he was unknown, he was not unfaithful. Thaddaeus went as a bond slave of Christ and he trusted that the Master was responsible for all the needs of the servant. It was a matter of total dependence of Jesus. The twelve left everything behind to follow Jesus without any promise of home or financial security. Yet they were content and faithful to the end.

From Thaddaeus we also learn the lesson that while people may not readily recognize our name, Jesus knows our name. In that wonderful tenth chapter of John, Jesus is identifying Himself as the "Good Shepherd." He is describing the personal, intimate relationship between the sheep and the shepherd. The entire conversation is remarkable, but none more so that His words, *"The sheep hear his voice, and he calls his own sheep by name and leads them out."* Most of us will not acquire great fame or recognition, but that matters not, for Jesus knows my name. He knows me now and he knew me before I was in my mother's womb. (Jeremiah 1:4-5) Like Thaddaeus, God desires not that we become famous, rather that we remain faithful.

Legend has it that Thaddaeus took the gospel into modern Turkey, and many miracles and ministry took place. That same legend says he died a martyr's death while there.

12

THOMAS: THE APOSTLE WHO WAS FRUSTRATED

Had Thomas taken any of the available personality assessments on the market today he would have been "off the charts" as an individual with both an analytic and pessimistic personality. Believe me, in my parallel careers as a pastor and financial planner, I encountered more than a few Thomases. Though not always, such individuals tend to present a stoic demeanor, always doing a deep dive into details and finding even the most minute possibilities of what might go wrong. In church it could be that person who tends to say, "We've never done it that way before." In financial services it is that person who sees every correction in market behavior to be the beginning of the next major economic recession. Thomas ranked up there with all those others who simply cannot believe what they cannot see for themselves. Let's face it, in Christianity that can be a significant problem. After all, the writer of Hebrews said, *"Now faith is the assurance of things hoped for, the conviction of things not seen."* While our culture says, "Seeing is believing," Christianity says, "Believing is seeing." That does not equate to taking a Pollyanna approach to life, but it does mean trusting matters of faith that are confirmed by the Word of God.

We have all said it, or least thought it about some other person. Sure, you have. You know certain folks that you have readily labeled a "doubting Thomas." What a way to have your name immortalized in history with a moniker like that…a doubter. I've known several of those doubting Thomases, and you have too. Truthfully, Thomas gets a bad rap. Yes, he had plenty of doubts relative to the death and resurrection of Jesus…. but so did all the other disciples. Think about it, I've had more than a few doubts and I am confident you have too.

We cannot deny that Thomas had a knack for seeing the downside in many things. In this book I dubbed him as the frustrated apostle. Given his personal disposition it would not have been unusual for him to experience bouts of despair, disillusionment, despondency…. which combined with his doubts led to feelings of frustration.

HIS RECORD

So, who is this guy, Thomas? We have no family records, although we do know that he had to have parents, and we know that somewhere out there he had a sibling. Like most of the disciples he had more than one name, and for Thomas that other name by which he was known was Didymus, which means "twin." In the book of Acts, we also find him referred to as Judas, which should not surprise us, given the popularity of that name in that culture. Yes, the Biblical record for Thomas is thin, but Jesus called him, appointed him, trained him and gave him a meaningful assignment as an apostle.

It is difficult to know a great deal about his character, but certain things can be surmised.

First, Thomas was bewildered. Toward the end of His earthly life Jesus was trying to explain what would happen. The men were not grasping what Jesus said. Jesus said, *"You know the way to where I am going."* Thomas didn't know what to think of Jesus' statement and was therefore bewildered. His question was factual, *"How can we know the way?"* Before we rail on Thomas for such a reply, remember, it is likely that others were wondering the same thing, they just didn't verbalize it. In the reply of Jesus, Thomas got more than he asked for.

Thomas was also a loyal person. In his commitment to Jesus, he was nothing like Judas. He may have doubted, but he was not a betrayer. The account in Acts lists Thomas among those who were faithful and still serving the Lord after his ascension.

As we have noted, Thomas was also a pessimist. He always saw the worst in any situation. A prime example of this is when Jesus decided to go to Bethany when Lazarus had died. Thomas seems to have taken a morbid outlook and approach to returning to a region where great opposition against Jesus existed. When other disciples resisted the idea of traveling back to that region, Thomas said, *"Let us also go so that we may die with him."*

However, the same conversation serves to demonstrate the level of commitment that Thomas had to Jesus. Even though he spoke in a manner that could be interpreted as moody and pessimistic, he was willing to go and die with Jesus. Thomas spoke as if to persuade the others to make the trip along with Jesus. Simon Peter said he was willing to go to prison and even die for Jesus, but then he changed his mind. Thomas made a similar statement and then backed it up by going to Bethany. Thomas fully expected to die in Bethany at the hands of the Jews.

Thomas talked the talk and walked the walk. Courage created a boldness in Thomas that took him directly into enemy territory. His life was on the line and yet he dared not be disloyal to Jesus. How sad that in the church of this age so few can be found who are willing to speak up, live courageously and march head-on, considering a culture that has become hostile and actively seeks to shame Christians for their values, virtues and convictions. Rather than focusing on a time of doubt in the life of Thomas, we should pray that we should be so courageous when so much is at stake.

HIS REBUKE

There did come that time in Thomas' life when he received a rebuke from the Lord. There are several reasons for the rebuke.

First, he was rebuked because of his absence. In John 20:24 Jesus made a post resurrection appearance to his disciples, but John noted this in his record, *"Now Thomas, one of the twelve, called the twin, was not with them when Jesus came."* Had Thomas been where he was supposed to be then he would have seen Jesus and would not have doubted the testimony of the apostles. When Jesus went to the cross, Thomas for some reason separated himself from the fellowship of the apostles. All the worry and trouble that came to Thomas, came because he was out of place...absent. Had Thomas been in his proper place of service alongside his fellow disciples, his difficulties and doubts would never have arisen, for he would have seen Jesus along with the others. For ages individuals have been critical of Thomas and called him "the doubter." However, empty seats and sparsely populated houses of worship on Sunday morning seem to suggest that many are still out of place and, like Thomas, fail to grasp the reality of a risen Savior and miss out on His glorious presence.

Thomas was also rebuked because he was skeptical. He had said that he was not able to believe unless he could see Jesus for himself. For this he received a rebuke from the Lord. Jesus said that a great blessing would be in store for all those who could believe without seeing. If the truth were known, all the apostles were probably doubters until they saw the Lord. After the crucifixion an interview with any apostle, if you could even locate them, would likely reveal an attitude of doubt and defeat.

Unbelief certainly brought about the rebuke of Thomas. Instead of accepting what he had been told in faith, and then praying for another opportunity to see Jesus, Thomas refused to believe. Unbelief is the sin that will carry untold millions to hell. Lack of faith is one thing that produces the unforgivable sin. Among believers, unbelief about the presence and power of Jesus is also an ever-present reality. Unbelief caused Thomas to miss out on fellowship with Jesus. Our absence, when He is present, will always short circuit what the Holy Spirit could have done had we been available to God.

Hebrews 10:19-25 is that Scripture which addresses the privilege and responsibility of every believer. Verse nineteen reminds us that it is with confidence that we can enter the "holy place." The writer refers to this privilege as a "new and living way." Wow! For believers God has an open-door policy. We have a standing invitation into the "Holy of Holies," which is the residence of God. In verse twenty the writer states that we have such confidence because the "curtain" no longer separates us from the presence of God. The writer refers to Jesus as the *"new and living way that he opened for us through the curtain."* That curtain that once hung in the tabernacle, and later in the temple, separating sinful man from Sovereign God, was torn open at the death of Jesus. In Ephesians 1:13 the apostle Paul said, *"But now in Christ Jesus you who were once far off have been brought near by the blood of Christ."*

The writer in Hebrews also tells us to live with conviction, *"… hold fast the confession of our hope,"* then he moves quickly to remind us of the importance of congregating with each other, so that we might encourage one another, living in the hope and promise of the return of Jesus Christ. I don't want to be absent and miss the presence and the glory of God. How about you?

HIS REWARD

The story of Thomas does not end with him a doubter, having missed out on the presence of Jesus. When the Lord finally appeared to Thomas, all his doubts and uncertainties vanished. He made the confession, *"My Lord and my God."* Thomas used the personal pronoun "my." That kind of confession will always result in redeeming faith.

It is significant to remember that Jesus did not condemn Thomas or scorn him. Instead, he invited Thomas to do exactly what he had wanted to do, to touch the scars and nail prints. Perhaps the reason Jesus did not condemn Thomas is because doubts are so human. May we never shy from inquiry, for from inquiry comes revelation.

The reward of Thomas came when he made the great discovery of the resurrected Lord, and it was based on a personal encounter with Christ.

It must be remembered that Thomas made his discovery in the presence of other believers. God's plan is for his people to be part of a great company and not be "Lone Ranger" Christians. It is likely that our service for Jesus can be done with greater ease and greater impact if we practice our faith in the fellowship of others with like faith.

His reward came as a result of that discovery, that indeed Jesus was alive. Oh, the thrill of such a moment, the thrill of the living, Lord Jesus. Notice, at first, he based the possibility of believing that Jesus was alive on what he could see. Oh, but now, he did not have to touch the nail prints. He knew he was in the presence of Jesus. The greatest reward of the Christian is to see Jesus after years of faithful service. Thomas passed through frustrations to a greater experience of faith which resulted in great blessing. In John 21:1-7 Jesus meets seven disciples on the banks of the Sea of Galilee. Thomas was in the group of seven. To no avail they had fished all night. From a distance, apparently too far to recognize, a man told them to change their fishing strategy. The result was an amazing catch of fish. John was the first to recognize that the man on the shore was Jesus, but it was Peter who dove in the water and was the first of the seven to reach Jesus. They had breakfast together that morning, and John 21:14 offers this commentary, "*This was the third time that Jesus was revealed to the disciples after he was raised from the dead.*" By this time Judas Iscariot was dead, so that leaves three disciples unaccounted for on that morning. Three disciples were elsewhere that morning. Five of those present are named, while two others are not named by the writer, John. However, and this is important, what we do know is that Thomas was one those seven men. Absent once, but not twice. Thomas held fast to his faith and with utmost confidence, conviction and commitment never again missed an opportunity to spend time with the Lord. When we meet Jesus, may the same be said of us.

13

JUDAS: THE APOSTLE WHO FORSOOK

I s it possible for an individual to align themselves with Jesus, affiliate with other followers of Jesus, and still be a hardened sinner? The apostle Paul seems to have such an experience in his ministry, for in 2 Timothy 4:9-10 he said, *"Demas, in love with this present world, has deserted me...."* So, yes, it is possible. Judas Iscariot was certainly one of those individuals. As early as the feeding of the five thousand, Jesus made a comment that one of the twelve would eventually betray him.

The story of Judas is one of the most confounding in the Bible. He was personally chosen by Jesus himself. He walked and talked with Jesus as did the other eleven disciples. He saw the same miracles, he heard the same sermons, he heard spiritual truth, he witnessed the dead live again. How could he walk away from the Son of God? Why would anyone do such a thing?

To this day the name Judas is associated with betrayal. Poor 'ole Thomas' name continues to be associated with doubting, ever boisterous Simon Peter is remembered for his denials, but Judas stands alone in his act of treachery. We know that Judas' father was named Simon, and that he hailed from Kerioth (translated Iscariot). Perhaps it is worth noting that Judas's hometown was in Judea, the southern region of the country. Jesus and the other eleven disciples were all from Galilee, which is in the northern region of the country. There existed a tension between the two regions, and of course the North and the South had a shared spite for the region of Samaria which lay in the middle region of the country. From all appearances Judas held some sort of leadership position within the disciples, but what happened? Did he feel like an outsider? How did a traitor, one so seemingly greedy and self-centered, make his way into the company of disciples?

The life of Judas apparently began as honorable, respected, and decent, but became vile and despised. There is no record of blemish or defect in Judas' life prior to his betrayal. It seems that he was held in high esteem by the other apostles and was seemingly a man of integrity, although after the fact it is recorded that he may have been taking money from the treasury of the disciples. There seems to have been no distrust from the other apostles in the upper room, which was right at the last.

In retrospect it seems that Judas was impatient, pessimistic, greedy, self-centered, moody, and even revengeful. He allowed the weak traits of a melancholic personality to dominate his life. He was more interested in fulfilling his own personal ambition rather than doing the will of God. He was motivated more by greed than grace.

HIS BACKGROUND

Little is known about the background of Judas, but Judas was a disciple in equal standing with the other eleven. It is not recorded when or how he became a disciple; he is just suddenly in the list. Speculation has him present at the preaching of John the Baptist in the wilderness. John seemed to draw the zealots to his preaching meetings. The initial meeting of Jesus and Judas is veiled for reasons that will never be known.

Judas enjoyed all the privileges and powers of all the other apostles. Jesus had warned that many would come in His name, but that many people would also be pretenders. Perhaps Jesus had in mind the confession of Judas when he told the parable of the sower and the seed. Could Judas be that seed that fell by the wayside, an example of someone who hears the Word and receives it, but because there was no depth to nourish its roots, it withers and dies? It was a shocking evening when Judas approached Jesus and placed the kiss of friendship on the cheek of Jesus, and immediately Jesus was arrested. The betrayer had struck. It appears that Judas had been included in all the activities of the group, and he had been appointed treasurer. How could such cruel desertion and betrayal arise from one who had spent so much time in the company of Jesus? As shocking as the action of Judas was, sadly, it is an action that is cruelly, and even callously, perpetrated on Jesus and his church on a regular basis. Rare is the pastor who has not had an experience like that evening near Gethsemane. What began as an evening of fellowship, dinner, the introduction of new doctrine (the Lord's Supper), singing and prayer, came to a crushing conclusion with the kiss of Judas.

HIS BELIEF

POLITICAL AMBITION. Judas was indeed a man with grave political ambitions and implications. The attachment of Judas to Jesus Christ was based on many wrong things, not the least of which was that expressed by a group of radical Jews who believed that their Messiah would come in the person of a military leader. Judas followed Jesus because his interpretation of John the Baptists sermon in the wilderness was an introduction of Jesus as political deliverer of the Jews. Judas was likely a member of the Sacarri and was seeking a way to end Roman domination over Israel. In Jesus, Judas was hoping for a general to raise up an army and deliver Israel. It is yet true that people follow Christ for wrong reasons. Judas had certainly made a mistake about the true nature of the kingdom Christ had come to establish.

PERSONAL AMBITION. As Jesus talked of a kingdom, thoughts of power must have danced through the head of Judas. As one of the twelve he would certainly have an important place when the "general" set up his kingdom. Judas thought his association with Jesus would bring him great personal gain. I have known individuals who join the church because they believe it will be "good for business." I have known a few who belonged to the church because it provided a political advantage. Others have joined because it provided them a sense of respectability in their community. The list is endless.

How tragic to see people attaching themselves to the name of Christ and His church for some selfish and personal gain.

HIS BARGAIN

CONVENIENT ARRANGEMENT. Judas was disappointed in the ministry of Christ, and the revengeful nature that he harbored rose to the forefront. Judas devised a devious plan to "pay back" Jesus for all his personal disappointments. He planned and waited for the right moment. Everything was deliberate. He found, in the Sanhedrin, a convenient and profitable way to rid himself of this Messiah, who had failed to meet the expectations of Judas.

COWARDLY ARRANGEMENT. The actions of Judas were those of a coward. He did his deed in the absence of a significant multitude. With no one around, it did not take much courage for Judas to do his dastardly work. He did it at night. His horrible deed was hidden in the darkness of night. The Bible says evil men love darkness, and Judas chose the night for the betrayal. He did it with a band of soldiers present. Judas saw to it that he had, as some say, "covered his own back." He did his deed with the authority of Rome behind him.

CALLOUS ARRANGEMENT. Judas used a kiss as a sign of betrayal. A kiss was normally the sign of close friendship. Even as Judas approached Jesus, the Lord called him "friend." Judas didn't have to give the kiss for the soldiers to identify Jesus. They asked his identity, and Jesus said, "I am He." Judas was willing to trade his soul for thirty pieces of silver, which by my calculation would be equal to about $600.00 today.

HIS BEWILDERMENT

A TESTIMONY OF TREACHERY. The betrayal by Judas came as no surprise to Jesus. As we have mentioned, Jesus spoke to his disciples regarding the fact that one of them would one day betray him.

A TORTURED CONSCIENCE. Judas was filled with guilt and remorse. He cried "I have sinned." There is no indication that he repented of his sin, only that he understood the full meaning of what he had done. In the Bible Judas is called the son of perdition. What a bewildered man Judas was. Like Judas, many remain bewildered about what to do with their consciences. Some try to silence their conscience with substances, or other substitutes, that lead only to addiction and misery. What, after all, is our conscience? At the simplest level it is our conscience that creates in us an awareness of right and wrong. It is also our conscience which testifies to our souls the very existence of God. Our conscience expresses our value system. I've heard it said, "Let your conscience by your guide." That sounds sweet, right? Yet, it could be deadly. A conscience is trustworthy only when that conscience is subordinate to Scripture and the Holy Spirit. Christians are bound only by what the Bible forbids or commands. To act against a biblically informed conscience is sin. The Bible has much to say about our conscience. We can have a pure conscience (Titus 1:15; 1 Timothy 1:5). Some will have a guilty conscience (1 Samuel 24:10). Sadly, some have a seared (insensitive) conscience (1 Timothy 4:2). It is certainly desirable to have a clear conscience (Romans 8:1; Hebrews 13:18; Acts 24:16). Some have a good conscience (1 Peter 3:16) while others have a weak conscience (1 Corinthians 8:7) Our conscience can speak (bear witness) to us (Romans 2:15). Thankfully a conscience can be purified (Hebrews 9:14). Some have a wounded conscience (1 Corinthians 8:12), and as we have seen in the case of Judas, one can have an evil conscience (Hebrews 10:22). So, before we dare allow our conscience to be our guide, let's put it to the Biblical test to ensure it is God, not our enemy, who is speaking through our conscience.

A TRAGIC END. Judas has his name eternally engraved as a traitor. My, what an epithet for a gravestone. His story serves to remind us that where our treasure is, our heart is also. Some might dare say that Judas had no choice, that he was somehow divinely elected as the one necessary (the means) to bring about God's predetermined plan. I certainly believe in the omniscience of God, but I also believe the Bible when it says, "*Whosoever will, may come.*" So, was salvation available to Judas? If so, when? I believe that even when Judas held that rope in his hand, intent on taking his own life, there was still that opportunity for his story to end differently. You see, there are two parallel tracks in the Bible, the divine sovereignty of God and human choice. In the divine sovereignty of the Bible everything is foreordained by God. Yet, in the Bible a person is fully responsible for all his or her actions. How can both of those be correct? Our minds can't fully grasp that, but "out-there" in the distance, like the two rails of the same train track, the two converge into eternity. I grieve when reading the New Testament, for I see many who met Christ, but like the so-called rich young ruler, they walk away from Jesus unchanged. I think of all those I have known in my life, especially in more than fifty years of ministry, who have been introduced to Jesus, but they walk away, unchanged. I think of those who served alongside me in ministry, who like Judas, turned their back on truth, and walked away. I pray that none who may read this book find such a tragic ending to their story.

14

PAUL: THE APOSTLE WHO WAS FEARLESS

Philosopher, scholar, rabbi, attorney- all accurate terms for Saul of Tarsus, who within the realm of Christianity came to be known as Paul the apostle. While truly all those things, it is much more likely that first century Christians thought of him as a brutal terrorist. His self-appointed mission was the obliteration of the early "Jesus movement." That fact is no more clearly seen than in the book of Acts where he attended, and approved of, the stoning death of Stephen. It is further seen in Acts that he acquired legal documents that provided him with authority to seek out, persecute, and even kill followers of Jesus Christ. On one of those terrorist missions something happened – something astonishing and transforming happened. On a roadside, in fact, in a ditch, Saul had a supernatural encounter with Jesus Christ that changed his life, and the very life of the early Christian church. His teaching and writing shaped church history and Christian thought and theology in a way like no other. Only Jesus himself commands more of our attention than does the apostle Paul.

Following his encounter with Jesus, Paul with his extrovert personality and his driver style of getting things done, moved on to be Paul the preacher, Paul the theologian, Paul the missionary, Paul the prolific writer, Paul the Christian apologist, Paul the soul-winner —Paul the Christian martyr. His grit and his zeal sent him and his fellow travelers on three extensive mission endeavors. God's favor and anointing was on him, and yet he was beaten multiple times and faced repeated rejection, near death experiences, being lost at sea, and numerous trips to prison, all for his faith. He once said, "*We are troubled on every side.*" Yet, of those many horrid experiences he said, "*We are perplexed, but not in despair, persecuted, but not forsaken; cast down, but not destroyed.*" With his abiding faith in God, and living in the assurance of the continual presence of the Holy Spirit, Paul was truly a remarkable and fearless apostle.

I once heard Dr. J. Vernon McGee say of Paul, "No place remained the same after Paul visited there. When Paul came to town it brought either revival or revolution."

WONDERFUL PEDIGREE

Few people in the New Testament were better educated than the apostle Paul. He had been taught by some of the brightest and best of his day. Most notably, Gamaliel. Gamaliel was a leader among the Jewish Sanhedrin and was himself the son and grandson of two of the most noted Jewish teachers in all of Judaism—Simeon ben Hillel and Hillel the Elder. Clearly, Paul received one of the finest educations available. Paul combined his education and heritage with a temperament that lent itself to a dogged determination which at times, prior to conversion, seems to have almost bordered on fanaticism. In a temperament analysis Paul would have had primarily the personality of the Choleric (Driver Social Style), combined with the Melancholy (Analytic Social Style). He was driven, strong willed, gifted, and perfectionistic. He, like others of the same temperament, was fond of making decisions for himself and others. He thrived on activity. But Pauls' activity always had a purpose. There was always the next crusade to take up. Fortunately for us, after his conversion Paul's internal traits drove him to become the most vocal, out front, spokesperson for Christianity. His analytical tendency is on full display in the book of Romans. The theological section of Romans – chapters 1-8—is rich, thorough, and reasonable.

Paul's educational background, supercharged by his personality, is incredible, but it is only one component of his pedigree. In Philippians 3:4-6 Paul describes his pedigree for his readers, *"Though I myself have reason for confidence in the flesh also. If anyone else thinks he has more reason for confidence in the flesh, I have more: circumcised on the eighth day, of the people of Israel, of the tribe of Benjamin, a Hebrew of Hebrews; as to the law, a Pharisee; as to zeal, a persecutor of the church; as to righteousness under the law, blameless."* Just so we are clear on the power of God to transform our temperament (personality) the next few verses describe how Jesus Christ had completely transformed this Hebrew of Hebrews. *"But whatever gain I had, I counted as loss for the sake of Christ. Indeed, I count everything as loss because of the surpassing worth of knowing Christ Jesus my Lord…that I may know him and the power of his resurrection, and may share in his sufferings, becoming like him in his death, that by any means I attain the resurrection of the dead."* Spoken like the true words of a transformed Choleric (Driver Social Style). As an aside, since one side of Paul's temperament is that of the Melancholy (Analytic Social Style), we should not be surprised to see the precise, almost accountant like, work of the apostle as he puts together a profit and loss statement of his life before Christ, and after Christ.

Within those verses Paul provides us with a clear outline of his pedigree.

- National heritage – circumcised on the eighth day. Circumcision had become by the first century, in which Paul lived, an important ritual. Yes, ritual. Its true meaning as a sign of God's covenant with His people had been lost to rules, religion, and rituals. Nonetheless, Paul before his conversion remained most proud of his association with this religious ritual. Ishmaelites were circumcised on the thirteenth day, but Jews were always circumcised on the eighth day. So it is that Paul reminds us of his proud heritage as a Jew.

- Religious heritage – Lee Greenwood has a song in which he boldly declares, *"I'm proud to be an American..."* In that song, *God Bless the USA,* Greenwood says that he loves America, and proclaims that from sea to sea and border to border, he lives in a great land. Paul certainly felt that way about Israel. However, Paul's love for Israel was more than a national love. When he made the declaration that he was of the stock of Israel, he was looking beyond the flag. In this statement Paul was attaching himself to the spiritual status associated with the name Israel. Israel was the spiritual name, the religious name, assigned to the Jewish people.
- Kingly heritage – The tribe of Benjamin was filled with nobility. Saul, the first King of Israel sprung from the tribe of Benjamin, as did Queen Esther, whose story is told in the Bible book that bears her name. The tribe of Benjamin was also known for its valor. They performed bravely and valiantly in battle against the enemies of Israel.
- Pure heritage – one of Paul's young associates and missionary companions was Timothy. In Acts 16 when Paul and Silas prepped for the second of Paul's missionary trips, they made a stop in the city of Derbe and met a fine young man named Timothy. Two of Paul's New Testament letters were written to Timothy, who became a church leader and pastored the church at Ephesus (modern day Turkey). Timothy had been nurtured in faith by his Jewish mother and grandmother. Luke, in writing Acts, thought it significant enough to include the fact that Timothy's father was Greek, not a Jew. Since Luke was a traveling companion of Paul at the time of this trip one might assume that Luke understood the struggle that existed in early Christianity between the Jews and those "dogs," the Gentiles. Luke full well understood that strife, and I have no doubt that he and Paul had many conversations about the topic of

being a pure Jew versus a Gentile coming into
Christianity. Paul boasted in Philippians that he was a
Hebrew of Hebrews.

- Legal heritage – Scripture makes it clear that Paul was
  both a Pharisee and a member of the elite Jewish ruling
  body known as the Sanhedrin. Both those groups were
  strict adherents of Jewish law. Jesus himself had
  numerous spirited encounters with the Pharisees, and of
  course, it was the Sanhedrin that sentenced Jesus to
  death as a "law" breaker. Paul was a student of the law
  and a protector of the law. He likely spent countless
  hours in the synagogue not only lecturing on, but also
  debating, the law. He would have practiced fasting, and
  he certainly would have been a tither. It was one of these
  debates in the synagogue in which another regular
  attender and debater by the name of Stephen so
  outraged the audience (including Saul of Tarsus) that he
  was taken outside and stoned to death.

Thankfully for us, and fortunately for Paul, as he describes in
Philippians, there came a day when all that pedigree meant little to
nothing. He found something of much greater importance and
value than all those religious and worldly accolades. Again, from
Philippians we hear Paul speak, *"I count everything as loss because of the
surpassing worth of knowing Christ Jesus my Lord."*

WARDEN OF THE PERSECUTED

Perhaps one of the most, if not the most, courageous witnesses for
Jesus Christ in the New Testament was a man we simply know as
Stephen. Our first glimpse of Stephen occurs in Acts 6 at a point in
the life of the early Christian church when a dispute arose between
two groups of individuals within the church. That dispute was over
how church resources were being spent, and over how ministry to
some church members appears to have been subpar. Those persons,
especially the widows – whom the church felt very responsible for,

but who were not a part of the more traditional Jews – were feeling neglected. The more traditional Jews who had become Christians held in low regard the Jewish Christians who came from a culture that was more Greek than Jewish. Their disdain for the Hellenistic members of the church had become obvious. The apostles needed to act, and they made a wise decision when they agreed among themselves that there needed to be a care plan for the daily needs of the fledging congregating. Yet, the rapid growth of the church dictated that they needed help in caring for many of the ministry tasks. They chose a group of seven servants to come alongside the apostles who would focus on the daily operation and ministry of the church. These men are called *deacons* (servant) here in Acts 6. A total of seven were chosen to serve as deacons, and one of them was Stephen, who was *"Full of grace and power, doing great wonders and signs among the people."* In other words, Stephen was a hands-on servant in his ministry, but he was also clearly an outspoken and energetic preacher of the gospel. It was his preaching that caught the attention of the Sanhedrin, of whom Saul of Tarsus was a member.

Beginning in Acts 6:9 a confrontation between Stephen and several members of the Sanhedrin took place, and the Bible indicates that Stephen outwitted and outdebated that group of detractors. Scripture states that Stephen spoke with wisdom given to him by the Holy Spirit. Stephen's adversaries, full of rage and seeking revenge, resorted to deception, and used false witnesses to make untrue claims about Stephen's message. The false arrest of Stephen opened the way for him to preach in the synagogue and his sermon was filled with the vision that God had given him for the Kingdom of God. Stephen envisioned the kingdom for all who would believe in Jesus Christ as the Son of God. The door "in" was not just for Jews, but Gentiles as well who would believe. The tipping moment came when Stephen said to his Jewish listeners in the Synagogue, *"You stiff necked people, uncircumcised in heart and ears, you always resist the Holy Spirit…"*

The angry response of those religious traditionalist was to apprehend Stephen, and they took him outside and began stoning him to death. Whereas Stephen was a valiant, courageous witness for Christ, this mob became a group of vicious, calloused witnesses to a crime. Acts 7:58 says, *"Then they cast him out of the city and stoned him. And the witnesses laid down their garments at the feet of a young man named Saul."* Then Acts 8:1 adds this commentary, *"And Saul approved of his execution."* Angered to no end by the preaching of Stephen, he was moved quickly to the place of his death. Yet, for only a moment, as if all the murderous shouts of his accusers were silenced by the Holy Spirit, we can hear Stephen speak just moments before his death, *"Lord Jesus, receive my spirit."* Then, resembling the words of Jesus from the cross Stephen said, *"Lord, do not hold this sin against them."* Without a doubt Stephen was one of the brightest, most Spirit filled young men that we shall ever meet in the New Testament. Perhaps, at least from our human perspective, he was destined to be the apostolic replacement for Judas, rather than Saul. Obviously, God had something else in mind. His tragic death, ending such a promising career in ministry, falls into that category of human events that are mind boggling, inexplicable, and humanly speaking feels irreconcilable with our faith. Saul may have brushed aside the words he had heard from the young preacher, but surely those words would soon come back to haunt him. Yet for the time being, Saul pressed on in his merciless quest against the church. In fact, in Acts 8:3 we have this record, *"But Saul was ravaging the church, and entering house after house after house, he dragged off men and women and committed them to prison."* Saul had become the warden of the persecuted, the prosecuted, the imprisoned, and yes, even the executed.

Saul, our consenting witness to the death of Stephen, secured legal documents that provided him with the authority to arrest and imprison any person he found in any city that belonged to *The Way*. (Acts 9:1-2) In his adopted mission to hinder, if not destroy, the rapid spread of the gospel seemed willing to use any violent means necessary to bring Jewish justice to any who dared name the name of Jesus.

WOUNDED PENITENT

Saul embarked on a wicked mission, as Acts 9 makes clear, *"But Saul still breathing threats and murder against the disciples of the Lord…"* Saul, the strong-willed Jew, was certain that those following "The Way" had been deceived by the stories being spread about Jesus. It seems the more determined and dangerous he became in his defiance, the more the gospel continued to spread. The fact he was traveling to Damascus with arrest warrants in his hand is evidence that the gospel had taken up residence there. Philip had recently encountered the man from Ethiopia, who upon being saved, took the gospel with him to the south. The intense efforts of Saul to thwart the spread of the gospel were failing. The gospel was out running Saul, and soon this militant defender of traditional Judaism would meet his match.

Saul's trip was interrupted when he encountered a weird and wonderful meeting. Weird, in that he saw and heard things that no one else saw or heard. Wonderful, in that he experienced a personal visit from the risen Christ, and wonderful in the fact that his conversion brought to Christianity an intellectual who provided us with deep theological truth, a firebrand of an evangelist who persisted in spreading the gospel, and one who modeled for us what a spirit filled life can accomplish in a single lifetime. Blinded and struck to the ground, Saul heard a voice – and when he asked who was speaking to him – the answer came, *"I am Jesus…"*

Jesus said next, *"…rise and enter the city, and you will be told what you are to do."* Saul could not have known it then, but he would eventually walk into a mystery, a mystery that he would declare in his letter to the Ephesians was, *"…made known to me by revelation… when you read this you can perceive my insight into the mystery of Christ, which was not made known to the sons of men in other generations as it has now been revealed to his holy apostles and prophets by the Spirit. This mystery is that the Gentles are fellow heirs, members of the same body, and made partakers of the promise in Christ Jesus through the gospel."* In Ephesians Paul is clearly talking about the revelation of the Church, of an all–inclusive church, filled with any and everyone who upon hearing the gospel repented of their sin, confessed Jesus as Lord, and who then became a member of the "body of Christ." Paul's conversion appears to have taken place around 33 A.D., and in 64 A.D., as a prisoner of Rome, Paul was executed for his faith. Rising from that roadside encounter, he walked and ministered for more than thirty years, growing more certain with the passing of each year that he had been called to preach and teach the gospel. It was his belief that upon hearing the good news, and walking in the light, others would become partakers and participants in the mystery.

WARRIOR IN PRAYER

The greatest heroes of faith in Scripture had an undeniable dependence on prayer. The prophets had a dependence on prayer. Women like Hannah and kings such as David and Solomon had a dependence on prayer. The apostles of the New Testament discovered that they too had a dependence on prayer. Even Jesus, the Son of God, demonstrated that he depended on prayer. In what we have come to refer to as the Lord's Prayer, in response to the disciples asking him to teach them how to pray, he provided a model that continues to provide us with the basic tenets of effective praying. (Luke 11:1-4) Andrew Murray, in his great "Collected Works on Prayer," reminds us that Jesus extends two significant invitations to us all. The first, in Matthew 11:28 is *"Come unto me."* The second is *"Abide in me,"* found in John 15:4. The first invitation invites us into a saving relationship with Jesus Christ. In repentance we confess our undone state (total depravity), ask for divine forgiveness, and move into a new state, what Paul describes in 2 Corinthians 5:17 as a new creation. The New Living Translation says, *"The old life is gone, a new life has begun."* One discovers that this new life is filled with joy and blessings, but it also has – from our human perspective – moments of pain, disappointment, loss, and even failure. That is where the second invitation comes into play, *"Abide in me."* Sadly, my experience has been that many who experience conversion never discover the secret of the spirit filled life. The secret, which is no secret at all, is to accept Jesus' invitation to abide with him. Many years ago, I pastored a church in a small town in Southwest Alabama. More than a few times one of the church members would say, "Preacher, why don't you come by and sit-a-spell?" Now, being a country boy myself I understood their request. They meant they wanted me to come to their house and stay long enough to get better acquainted. We might sit on the front porch and have a glass of sweet tea or lemonade. Or we might sit at the kitchen table and have a piece of pie and a glass of milk. For me, those "sit-a-spell" times were priceless. I learned who they really were, how they processed information, what their relationships were really like, how they felt about the church, and how they related to Jesus. They also taught me many valuable lessons about life and pastoring. I was gradually changed for the better by those encounters. That is what Jesus was talking about when he said, *"Abide in me."* Only when we make a habit of stopping and sitting down with Jesus will we become truly acquainted with him, and only then will we learn the blessing of peace and joy, no matter our outward circumstances.

Paul understood that, and from his continual sitting and abiding with Christ his remarkable prayer life developed in knowing and praying the heart of the Father:

- Paul prayed for our soul's encouragement – In the opening of his letter to the church at Rome he said, *"For God is my witness, whom I serve with my spirit in the gospel of his Son, that without ceasing I mention you always in my prayers..."* (1:8) We believers need hope and encouragement, and Paul not only understood that, but he prayed that faith would rise up in every believer and that they would find the encouragement needed to find victory in Jesus.

- Paul prayed that we might find spiritual wisdom – *"I do not cease remembering you...in my prayers, that the God of our Lord Jesus Christ...may give you a spirit of wisdom and of revelation in the knowledge of him, having the eyes of your hearts enlightened...."* (Ephesians 1:16-18)

- Paul prayed that we would be strong in the spirit – "*For this reason I bow on my knees before the Father...that according to the riches of his glory he may grant you to be strengthened with power through his Spirit in your inner being...having strength to comprehend with all saints what is the breadth and length and height and depth, and to know the love of Christ that surpasses knowledge....*" (Ephesians 3:14-19)
- Paul prayed that we would always be sincere in our faith – "*And it is my prayer that your love may abound more and more, with knowledge and all discernment...so be pure and blameless... filled with the fruit of righteousness...*" (Philippians 1:9-10)
- Paul prayed that we might live worthy of our shared inheritance – to the Colossian Christians he encouraged them to live "...*so as to walk in a manner worthy of the Lord, fully pleasing to him.*" Paul went on to remind them that they had every reason to be filled with joy and thanksgiving, "...*giving thanks to the Father who has qualified you to share in the inheritance of the saints of light....*" Paul told them that "...*from the day we heard, we have not ceased to pray for you.*" (1:9-12)

Scripture reveals that the apostle Paul was tireless in his prayer life. Endless hours were spent praying for churches, individual believers, and even unbelievers. My own mother emulated Paul in her prayer life. Many today, known and unknown, have benefited from her hours of time in conversation with God. The great need of the church today is to have such warriors who never stop, who never surrender, and who refuse to be squelched in matters that need taking before the Lord.

Like Annie Hawks (1872) in her prayer of supplication and surrender – a prayer that we now sing before the Lord...

> "*I need thee, O I need thee;*
> *Every hour I need thee!*
> *O bless me now, my Savior,*
> *I come to Thee.*"

This great apostle was called of God to preach, and Paul understood that each time a preacher stands with an open Bible in their hand, and says, "Thus says the Lord," hell stands at attention. The forces of darkness rise to fight each time the light of the gospel is preached. Paul understood the struggles of warfare in preaching, but he knew he must preach, *"For necessity is laid upon me. Woe to me if I do not preach the gospel."* Furthermore, the New Testament bears out that Paul was a writer with purpose. There is complete agreement that Paul wrote no fewer than thirteen of the books in the New Testament, and many add the book of Hebrews to that list of thirteen. Prolific, personal, provocative, prayerful, and perhaps at times even pungent, are terms that aptly define his unparalleled style and stamina. Finally, as seen in 2 Timothy 4:6-8, when Paul knew that his execution was near, he chose illustrative language to express his thoughts about life and death. As the end approached, he was willing to be poured out, as he called it. As he sat in the dark and dank jail cell, he was reflecting on that Damascus Road experience, now thirty years in the past. What a day that had been when his life was so radically transformed, and now what a day it was about to be, for Paul was now ready to be offered. His life would be offered, poured out like a drink offering to the ancient gods. Only for Paul, his life was being poured as a sacrifice, much as was the Mosaic offerings poured over the sacrifices being offered to God. Paul was not desperate nor despondent. His words reveal his heart, *"I have fought the good fight, I have finished the race. I have kept the faith. Henceforth there is laid up for me the crown of righteousness, which the Lord, the righteousness judge, will award me on that Day, and not only to me but also to all who have loved his appearing"* (2 Timothy 4:7-8).

15

MATTHIAS: THE FORGOTTEN APOSTLE

reviously, in the opening chapter of this book, it was
mentioned that a formal listing of the twelve apostles appears
four times in the Bible. Three of the Gospels, along with Acts, bear
the names on a list, with minor variations in the order of the list,
with the exception that the name of Peter is first in all four lists. In
this chapter it is the list provided us from the hand of Dr. Luke that
takes center stage. No, not the list in his gospel, but the list that Luke
furnishes us in the book of Acts. It is as though Luke, owing to the
horrific act of betrayal by Judas, took an eraser and scrubbed Judas'
name from the honor roll of apostolic appointment.

A MEETING ARISES

Acts 1:12-26 presents a critical time for these disciples, who for three
years had given up everything they knew and had in order to follow
Jesus. They had witnessed the cruel death of Jesus on a Roman
cross. One of their own, Judas had taken his own life. They then
were allowed to spend some resurrection time with Jesus, but now
He had ascended to heaven, and now what would they do?
Fortunately, for them and for us, they did just what Jesus had told

them to do – wait. These once twelve, but now eleven, followers of Jesus huddled in Jerusalem. Their initial response to the death of Jesus had been chaotic. Some went home, some hid, some locked themselves behind closed doors, and some even went back to fishing. But now, they waited!

Luke indicates that the eleven disciples were joined by others, including the mother of Jesus, and it is clear that Luke was in the meeting. Peter, ever the leader, moved to take charge of the meeting, and I can only wish that in times of not knowing what to do next, that I had always followed the pattern of the group meeting in the upper room. Three things jump from verses fourteen and sixteen. There was unity, there was prayer, and there was attention given to Scripture. The experience we simply refer to as "Pentecost" was imminent and the fire of heaven was soon to fall and the Holy Spirit was about to usher believers into a new dimension, a new age – the age of the Church. I am convinced that Pentecost was realized because those people first did something – they obeyed the Lord (verse 4) – which they seasoned with prayer and Scripture – which brought them into unity (one accord). That formula still works today. Want to see a mighty move of God? Want to see revival in the church? Want to see lives changed? When we make His plans our plans, and we pray and stay true to the Word of God, unity will arise and heaven will come down, and glory will fill our souls. Our meetings, whatever we choose to call them (church, Life groups, Sunday School, Small groups), need less of us and more of Him.

A MAN ARISES

Peter, having assumed leadership of the meeting, recommends that a successor to Judas needs to be appointed. Peter quotes David by saying, *"Let another take his office."* Peter noted that it was the Holy Spirit who led David to remark concerning the one who would betray Jesus, how he would die, and that he would need to be replaced. Peter is using Psalm 69, a messianic Psalm, and is also quoting from Psalm 109:8, (*"May his days be few, and another take his place"*) when he broaches the idea of replacing Judas. Peter provides graphic details into the death of Judas. Peter also declares that Judas had gone to his own place (hell).

The methodology chosen for the selection of the apostolic replacement has created much conversation, and even controversy. There are those, of course, who are of the opinion that Peter and the others were too hasty in electing a replacement. Still others question the casting of lots as the method used for the selection process. Some cry that they resorted to a pagan process. However, remember, casting lots was an accepted method in the Old Testament and would have been accepted as an honorable thing for the group to do. Even the so-called Robe of Judgment, which is mentioned in Exodus, and worn by the Priest, had little pockets sewn in the robe, and little stones were kept in those pockets. Strange, huh? Why? The stones were rolled and used to determine the will of God. So, Peter and the others were simply following protocol that had been passed down through the centuries.

Peter also outlined the qualifications for the person who would join their apostolic ranks. In Acts 1:21 he said, "*So one of the men who have accompanied us during all the time that the Lord Jesus was with us....*" So, the first qualification was that the new apostle needed to be someone who had been with Jesus from the early days of His ministry. He would need to be someone who had kept close company with Jesus and would thus have first-hand knowledge of all that Jesus had said and done.

The apostolic successor would need to be one who dated back to John the Baptist, "*...beginning from the baptism of John...*" Peter and the others had been regular attendees at many of John's gatherings in the desert. John preached about one who was coming to save Israel. That caught the full attention of those like Peter who longed for freedom from the oppressors, who looked forward to a Messiah who would be their deliverer. Peter believed any new apostle should come from the ranks of those who had seen and heard the Baptist.

Finally, Peter said, "*These men must become with us a witness to His resurrection....*" These qualifications created a pool of qualified individuals, and from that pool two men were selected as finalists for the position. Those two candidates were Joseph called Barsabas, surnamed Justus, and Matthias. It is an interesting note that later in the life of the church, Judas Barsabas and Silas were sent by the Jerusalem church to accompany Paul and Barnabas to Antioch. This Judas is believed to have been the brother of Joseph Barsabas. Clearly, both these brothers were deeply committed to Christ and shared in the commission to go make disciples. After prayer, the lots were cast and Acts 1:26 says the lot fell on Matthias, and he was thus appointed an apostle.

A MYSTERY ARISES

The actions of Peter and the other apostles in the upper room have been a point of question and debate for centuries. There are many Bible teachers who insist that while Peter was sincere in what he did, he was nonetheless acting out of his own accord, not that of the Holy Spirit. If that were true, what motivation might Peter have had that would cause him to act so soon after the death of Judas and the ascension of Jesus. One thought surely rests in the thinking of all the followers of Christ, and that was that Jesus spoke often to his followers of the Kingdom that was coming. In many ways it is possible that Peter was still thinking in terms of an earthly Kingdom, and above all else they believed that Jesus' teaching pointed to an imminent Kingdom…one which would arrive any day now. In Matthew 19:28 Jesus had said, "*Truly I say to you, in the new world, when the Son of Man will sit on his glorious throne, you who have followed me will sit on twelve thrones, judging the twelve tribes of Israel.*" Who can blame Peter for believing that Jesus was returning soon, and upon returning His throne would be established, and the twelve apostles would each sit on a throne? Believing that, Peter felt an urgency to fill the void left by Judas' betrayal and death. They did not want Jesus returning to find an unoccupied throne.

There is an equally good argument that Peter was following the plan of God in filling the vacant seat, and that the selection of Matthias was a spiritually valid election. Some excellent teachers point to the fact that beyond his election Matthias is never mentioned again in the Bible. There is no record of any missionary travels. None of his sermons are recorded, nor his name ever mentioned in affiliation with any church. While that is true, the same can be said for many of the original twelve apostles. Clearly Matthias had been a loyal, faithful follower of Jesus Christ – and had thoroughly given himself to the ministry of serving alongside Jesus and the others. Remember, there were far more than the twelve who traveled with Jesus. On one occasion we know that at least seventy of his most ardent followers were sent out to preach and heal.

There are no conclusive answers in the matter – it remains a mystery. What is not a mystery is that all of those in that upper room, and thousands who came after them, did what they were called by the Master to do - turn the world upside down for Christ.

16

THE GOOD NEWS—TELL IT
FORCEFULLY

Had I been among those early hearers of Jesus, I have often pondered how I might have responded. Again and again, Jesus said to many who saw and heard him, "Come follow me." In the more complete version of that simple invitation He said, *"Come follow me and I will make you fishers of men."* Among His early followers were several fishermen, and I am certain they understood at least some, if not all, that Jesus meant in that invitation. Jesus was not only calling them for a life of discipleship, but was also implying that He had a specific plan for their lives. A plan that would involve reporting for duty on the front lines of the war that rages between heaven and earth. The apostle Paul makes it clear in Ephesians 6:10-12 that the war is real, *"Finally, be strong in the Lord and in the strength of his might. Put on the whole armor of God, that you might be able to stand against the schemes of the devil. For we do not wrestle against flesh and blood, but against the cosmic powers over this present darkness, against spiritual forces of evil in heavenly places."* Surely, we recognize the dark clouds that have gathered above us and against us. Yet, we are not left defenseless. Here in Ephesians Paul goes on to describe the implements of war that he has put at our disposal. Combine that with Paul's words in 2 Corinthians 10:3 *"The world is unprincipled...the world doesn't fight fair. But we don't fight our battles that way – never have and never will. The tools of our trade are not for marketing or manipulation, but they are for demolishing that entire massively corrupt culture. We use our powerful God-tools for smashing warped philosophies, tearing down barriers erected against the truth of God, fitting every loose thought and emotion and impulse into the structure of life shaped by Christ. Our tools are ready at hand for clearing ground of every obstruction and building lives of obedience into maturity."* (MSG) Don't you see, the enemy has schemes, but we have God tools, made for tearing down the opposition of our enemy.

Having graduated high school in June 1967, I had my eighteenth birthday in July 1967. Our nation was at war in Vietnam, which did not end until March 1973 when the U.S. withdrew its troops from Vietnam. The official end, as proclaimed by Congress, did not come until April 1975, when the last few American troops were pulled from Vietnam. At its high point more than 550,000 American troops were in Vietnam, and more than 58,000 Americans had lost their lives. In September 1967 I received a letter from what is known as the Selective Service System. The letter informed me that I was to report for military service, which for those in my vicinity began at the induction center in Montgomery, Alabama. As I left the hearing test I was taken by a corpsman to a room with no windows, a wall clock, and a set of climbing stairs. I assumed everyone was in a little room like the one I sat in...and boy, did I sit. The clock on the wall told me that I had been in that little room for almost an hour without seeing another soul. Finally, a man in a business suit entered the room and introduced himself as a cardiologist who had been called over to check me out. After running countless times up and down those stairs, he told me that I was being disqualified for military service because of a heart murmur. Several hundred of us had entered that facility early that morning. I never recognized any of the others in our group, and I often wondered what happened to the other hundreds who arrived there on that day.

I can only remember one other time that I was told that I was disqualified. In a high school track meet at which I easily won a 220-yard dash for the County Championship, only to have an official tell me that my foot stepped on the line that separated the running lanes, and I was therefore disqualified. A race and the medal that came with winning, which I thought I won, was going to be in some other runner's possession. The apostle Paul, who loved sports, had several analogies about the importance of training, endurance and working so as to never be disqualified.

Making the decision to answer the call of Jesus comes with expectations, requirements for participation, training, discipline, and desire. Paul had much to say about getting into and staying in the game. Mind you, Paul did not use sports analogies to suggest that our salvation, that is regeneration, is somehow dependent on how we work, prepare, and how well we perform. New Testament Scripture is clear on that matter, "...*by grace you have been saved...for by grace you have been saved by faith. And this is not of your own doing, it is the gift of God, not a result of works, so no person may boast*" (Eph. 2:5,8-9). After all, that is the good news that all of us have the responsibility to pass along to others. Telling the good news is our primary way of answering the call of Jesus. To that point Paul makes this statement, "*But we have this treasure in jars of clay, so that we may show the surpassing power belongs to God and not to us*" (2 Corinthians 4:7). That treasure is the good news, the gospel, and the jars of clay are you and me. Every Christian has been entrusted with this treasure. It resides in us and has since the day we asked Jesus Christ to forgive our sins and to save us.

Paul's analogies from the sports arena are primarily applicable to our lives after our salvation. One of my favorite examples of this is found in Hebrews 12:1-2, "*Therefore, since we are surrounded by so great a cloud of witnesses, let us lay aside every weight, and sin which clings so closely, and let us run with endurance the race that is set before us.*" Our practices for the track team often consisted of running for several miles wearing a weighted vest along with weights on our ankles and wrists. However, I can assure you that when we went to participate in a track meet against other schools, we wore no extra weights. The weights were for training, but never for participating. The Christian life is one of training, exercise, discipline, and endurance. At the end of his life Paul said this of his pending death, "*I have fought the good fight, I have finished the race, I have kept the faith"* (2 Timothy 4:7). Like us, Paul had many flaws in his life, but he knew that his position in Christ was based on the completed work of Christ at Calvary, not on how many or how few flaws could be found in Paul's life. I am going to paraphrase what Paul said in Philippians 3:13-14, "I am not looking back at what is behind me, instead I choose to look straight ahead toward the finish line, for at the finish line Jesus will be there to meet me with the greatest prize of all." In Christ, we all win! In Christ no one is disqualified! No one!

GREAT COMMISSION CHURCHES

Most Christians and church goers have some degree of familiarity with the "Great Commission." This commission represents some of the parting words of Jesus to his disciples before he ascended back to heaven. The Great Commission is the heart and soul of all acts of evangelism and mission activities of individual believers and local churches. The commission is the final recorded directive from Jesus, and it held great significance to those early followers, and we should never lose sight of its significance for all of us. It is a divine directive that demands of disciples that we operate through the power of the Holy Spirit in dispensing he good news. After all, the word gospel means good news. Most of us who grew up attending church learned, either in Sunday School or Vacation Bible School, the rendering found in Matthew 28:19-20, *"Go therefore and make disciples of all nations, baptizing them in the name of the Father, the Son and the Holy Spirit, teaching them to observe all that I have commanded you. And behold, I am with you always, to the end of the age."*

To broaden the scope of your appreciation for and understanding of the Great Commission you will want to read the other three sets of Scriptures that relates to this commission. Read Mark 16:15-18, Luke 24:44-49, John 20:19-23, and Acts 1:8. By combining chapter 15 and 16 of Mark we can catch a fast moving, factual account of the last hours of Jesus, as well as the importance of the time He spent with His disciples prior to His ascension back to heaven.

It is Finished – The Crucifixion

The Gaithers released a powerful gospel song with the title, "It is Finished." Among its marvelous lyrics are the words, *"There's a line drawn through the ages – on that line stands that old rugged cross – on that cross a battle is raging – for the gain of a man's soul or it's loss...."* Wow, a battle with high stakes. Our very soul was on the line that day that Jesus Christ was brutalized and crucified.

The cross was a place of unspeakable suffering. If nothing else, death by crucifixion was brutal. It was a popular form of capital punishment used by the Romans and other nations in ancient Europe. We must never forget that in the face of such horrific torture Jesus declared that his life was not being taken (by Romans or Jews); rather, he was giving his life. I deserved to be on that cross. Jesus did not. Yet, he voluntarily bore the guilt and shame created by me, so that I would not have to experience that myself. On the human level Jesus experienced the physical pain associated with such a death, but he also suffered the psychological and emotional pain of such torture. Yet, the greatest pain of all was the pain of sin – all our sin, past and present. In Gethsemane the agony of what faced him caused blood vessels to erupt, resulting in blood seeping through his skin. The execution itself was barbaric, so much so that soldiers would typically speed along death by breaking the legs of those being executed in order that the weight of their own body would crush their lungs and end the execution.

The cross was also a place of great sacrifice. Mark 15 records the words of one of the soldiers attending the crucifixion, *"Truly, this was the Son of God"* (Mark 15:39). Philippians 2:5-8 makes clear the cost of this sacrifice, *"...Christ Jesus, who though he was in the form of God, did not count equality with God a thing to be grasped, but made himself nothing, taking the form of a servant, being born in the likeness of men. And being found in human form, he humbled himself by becoming obedient to the point of death, even death on a cross."* What sacrifice!

It Is Finished – The Conquest

Death and the grave were no match for Jesus. I suggest a study of Chapters 9 and 10 of Hebrews to get the full picture of how it was a very resounding victory for believers. There was first the borrowed grave into which the body of Jesus was laid (to accommodate Jewish burial customs). His resurrection from that grave brought us the assurance that the price of our redemption was now fully paid. Furthermore, the death and resurrection of Jesus opened full access to God. While it remains true that Jesus is our mediator, the writer of Hebrews also tells us that we now have access to the throne room of God. What's the big deal about that? You no longer are required to have a priest to make an offering for you, you no longer are dependent on the prayers of another person; you are a priest. You and I have direct access to God, and prayer takes us right through the open door. We are fully connected (reconciled) to God through Christ.

It Is Finished – The Commission

Here we are with that term once again – Commission. Soldiers are commissioned. Ambassadors are commissioned. Police officers are commissioned. The Oxford dictionary defines commission as an *instruction, command or duty to a person or group of people; to be officially charged with a particular function.*

This commission was first extended to early disciples, and not just those first twelve called by Jesus. Following the ascension of Jesus (Acts 1) at least 120 people gathered and strategized as to what was to happen next. They took seriously the command of Jesus to take their good news message across the world. Later chapters in Acts reveal what happens when a group of saved people get together (can you say church). Dr. Luke recorded those monumental evangelistic and missionary results. The first gathering, at which Peter preached, resulted in 3,000 people turning to Christ. A few pages further in Acts that number had grown to 5,000 then 8,000 and finally the outpouring of the Holy Spirit on the preaching of these commissioned members of God's army had grown to what Luke simply called myriads.

The commission is yes, for pastors, evangelists, and missionaries. We thank God for all of them. However, the commission to make disciples is for every Christian, not just the "professionals." It is not a suggestion...it is a mandate. I think Rev. Paul B. Smith of Canada summed up why our churches have become weak and too often powerless skeletons, dead and dry and disappearing. He said, *"The trouble with most Christians is that they never hitched the power of God to their everyday lives."*

President Roosevelt referred to the unimaginable bombing of Pearl Harbor by the Japanese as *"A day that will live in infamy."* It was and is. On the other side of the world Japanese Admiral Isoruko Yamamoto wrote in his diary, *"I fear all we have done is awaken a sleeping giant and fill him with a terrible resolve."*

The church is a sleeping giant, capable of doing once again what was recorded of those early disciples in Acts 17:6. The disciples were brought before authorities for disturbing the peace (false charges; it was really about the money). Yet, it is vital to pay attention to how the charge was worded, *"These who have turned the world upside down have come here also."* There are more than 800 churches in the county I live in. There are some very good churches here, but none of them are in danger of being charged with turning our city upside down for Jesus, much less the world.

When will we see the church aflame for Christ? The writer of Hebrews warned about the need to pay much closer attention (2:1) lest we suddenly realize that we have drifted from the moorings of preaching the Word, praying under the anointing of God, giving generously where money is spent reaching the lost and taking the Great Commission seriously. Like Ephesus, will we return to our first love? Are we tolerating false doctrine like Smyrna? Are we hung up on ecclesiastical order as was Pergamos? Have we become a hotbed of heresy as did Thyatira? Perhaps we as a church have become like Sardis, living in the glory days of the past, but currently dead with no cultural relevance. Or maybe the wonderful, willing Philadelphia Church, ready to do whatever God asked, but they lacked the resources to do it? A great many churches are represented by the church at Laodicea. They had plenty of resources, but Jesus brought this charge against them, *"I know your works; you are neither cold nor hot. So, because you are lukewarm...I will spit you out of my mouth"* (Revelation 2:15).

These short messages to these seven churches wrap up with a strong word applicable to almost every church I know, *"Behold, I stand at the door and knock. If anyone hears my voice and opens the door, I will come in...*(Rev.2:20).

Will you open the door? He knocks on the door of the heart of the lost, hoping to bring salvation. He knocks on the heart of the believer, hoping to bring spiritual renewal and recommitment for the individual. He knocks on the door of the heart of every church, hoping to be invited in...and when that happens...we will call it revival.

It is time to open the door and stand up and be the church. We have marching orders given under the authority of heaven and earth. It is estimated at the time of this writing that 3.2 million people have never even heard the name of Jesus. Jesus succinctly summarized the issue when he said, *"Time is short, and laborers are few."* We are all called to task. Some will sow the seeds of the gospel, knowing that some seed will fall on hard soil, rocky soil that will never grow anything. Some seed will be choked out by weeds thus guaranteeing no harvest. Some seed will seem to be producing a vibrant plant, but soon it's showing signs of wilting because the shallow roots have doomed the plant from the start. Thankfully, there is also some good ground. That good ground will allow the roots to dig deeply into the soil, providing life-giving nourishment and moisture.

It Is Finished - The Call

In First Corinthians Paul said, *"...for we are all God's fellow workers."* We must never forget we are called to sow gospel seeds. Some of us will sow seeds while others will water the seeds, but never forget, the harvest is the work of God. We have a calling, an assignment to take the good news to every person, every community, and every nation. Early on, to person after person, Jesus Christ said *"Follow me."* What has been your response?

My own call to ministry came about through an experience I alluded to early in this book, a disqualification. Graduating from high school in 1967, I had no real sense of what my life was to become. My answer to avoiding being drafted into the Army was to join the Army. Looking back, I realize that I was very naïve to think that joining, rather than being drafted, would ensure the opportunity to select my MO (Military Occupation). Frankly, in 1967 with the Vietnam War in progress, the infantry was the most likely landing place. Because I had excellent typing skills, I had been told I would become a "clerk typist." Whether with a rifle or a typewriter, it was not meant to be. As I have already stated, I was disqualified for military service due to a heart murmur. During the ensuing months I began to sense God calling me into ministry. As a teenager I had preached several times in our church on youth Sunday. Because of that preaching experience I was invited by other pastors in the county to fill in for them during times of their absence. Those opportunities began to increase, and those opportunities when combined with my experience with the Army, it began to dawn on me that might very well be God's way of getting my attention. On May 15, 1968, the church of my childhood and youth approved my licensing as a Minister of the Gospel. My ordination as a minister followed shortly thereafter. I am retelling that part of my personal journey with God because we have reached the entire purpose of this book. Yes, as we peek into the life experiences of the early apostles, it is hopefully a book of encouragement and enlightenment, but most of all I hope it brings us all to a moment of confrontation. Remember, all we believers are given that same call of *"Come follow me."* God has the same expectation of us now, as He did for those first disciples. That is, affirmatively answer the call of Jesus.

In his marvelous book "Spiritual Disciplines for the Christian Life," Donald Whitney reminds us of the purpose of practicing the spiritual disciplines. Those disciplines include, of course, time in the Bible, praying, fasting, worship, giving, solitude….and, serving. Some might ask, "Why bother with those disciplines?" For me it is simple. The U.S. military demands discipline from its troops; should God's army be any less prepared? Discipline requires practice (doing and doing again). Paul states in 1 Timothy 4:7, *"…discipline yourself for the purpose of godliness…."* Jesus spent three years training those apostles, as well as many other disciples, for the purpose of godliness. You and I have a calling that requires those same disciplines to be practiced in our lives, not the least of which is service. The assignment and discipline of service is not for a special few; it is for every believer. I received an exemption from service in the military for a medical reason. There are no exemptions from service in the Kingdom of God. Every believer is equipped and empowered (by the Holy Spirit) and expected to serve.

I could have easily titled this chapter "Beyond the Apostles," because that is the entire premise of this book. With the apostles as our model for service, we must fully engage, as both individuals and collectively as churches. Serve we must…and serve now!

Beyond the apostles, the New Testament is replete with examples of men and women and couples who heard the call of Jesus to follow…and they said yes. Hebrews 11 contains a list of names of many who faithfully served God. However, it also reminds us that many of those names will not be known until we reach heaven. Some of the other names we do know from the New Testament include Lazarus; James and Jude, the brothers of Jesus; Timothy; Titus; Philemon; Onesimus (who was a slave); Barnabas; Epaphroditus; Silas; and John Mark. We dare not forget the great missionary couple, Priscilla and Aquila. The great leaders and followers among the women included Mary Magdalene, the sisters of Jesus (Matthew 13:35), Mary and her sister Martha, Lydia, Dorcas, Phoebe, and so many others.

Those apostles, along with all those other names I have included, were alive during the first century. We remember their faith and use their example to encourage us. But is that enough? Twenty centuries have passed since they all contributed to turning the world upside down with the gospel. It is time for the rest of us to join Isaiah and say, *"Here am I, send me."*

AFTERWORD

To this day, much the same way that the people in this book did, Christians continue to do exactly what Jesus asked of them, *"Take up my cross, and follow me."* Why? Why, in many instances are we willing to leave family, the familiar and even fortune behind to answer yes, and follow the call of Jesus?

"And all these, though commended through their faith, did not receive what was promised, since God had provided something better for us, that apart from us they should not be made perfect (Hebrews 11:40). This verse appears at the end of chapter eleven, in which the writer has provided a long list of heroes and heroines, who all believed a promise and were willing to travel to unknown places, engage hostile cultures, endure unspeakable atrocities, all for an unseen promise. That same chapter of Hebrews begins with a definition of the faith required for such trust, *"Now faith is the assurance of things hoped for, the conviction of things not seen. For by it the people of old received their commendation (good report)."* Though not yet realized, their faith gave them confidence to look beyond present realities and see the promises realized in the future tense. That is exactly what those early disciples of Jesus did, after all, Jesus said to them, *"I go to prepare a place for you…and I will come again for you."* That promise became the compelling force behind the rapid

expansion of the early church. A group of ordinary men and women were given an outsized assignment, and with faith and extraordinary resolve, they set about turning the world upside down for Jesus.

That verse in Hebrews confirms the "why" of evangelism: missions and the local church. *Since God had provided something better for us…."* That something that awaits us is what Paul meant when he said, *"…what no eye has seen, nor ear heard, nor the heart of man imagined, what God has prepared for those who love him – these things God has revealed to us through the Spirit."* By faith we see the unseen. It is those glimpses of the glory of God that compel us to action, calm our anxieties, claim our allegiance and capture our attention. Eleven of those first disciples took a path that led them to see the unseen, to do the seemingly impossible, to believe the promise, and to stand firm in their faith. The threat of torture and even death did not dampen their faith nor deter them from fulfilling their calling and commitment to Christ. For those listed in Hebrews eleven, their faith was a matter of looking forward to Messiah. For those in this book, their faith was in a present reality (Jesus, God in the flesh) with a future fulfillment of the promise. The apostle John gave this testimony in his first letter, *"That which…we have heard, which we have seen with our eyes, which we looked upon and have touched with our hands…."* John is saying that Jesus was, for him and his disciple companions, a present reality. He went on to say, *"…that which we have seen and heard we proclaim to you, so that you too may have fellowship with us…."* John was saying that Jesus was real, and his promises are real. That created not only faith, but also fire, in their souls. That fire was stoked by the Holy Spirit, and no obstacle the enemy threw across their path was going to hinder them from proclaiming what they had seen and heard. The grand glory of their story is this…the religious establishment of Judaism, the smug intelligence of the Greeks, and the mighty military of the Romans, all stood across the path of the church. Any institution designed by man would have stopped in its tracks. Yet, the church marched on…person after person, town after town, nation after nation. The church on trial became the church triumphant. The church was built one living stone at a time, with each stone cemented to the next by the blood of saints who refused to deny Jesus, who refused to bow before kings, who just kept telling the story.

Today, sadly, Christians and the church have been belittled and verbally battered by a hostile culture that seeks to silence not only the church, but any person who disagrees with political philosophies that seek to disrupt families, seize fortunes, destroy freedoms and silence God's people. How did we get here? The answer lies in the premise of this book. Jesus is calling, a path is provided, and a promise is made, *"If my people, who are called by my name humble themselves, and pray and seek my face and turn from their wicked ways, then I will hear from heaven, and will forgive their sin and heal their land"* (2 Chronicles 7:14). Our churches, our communities, and our country have wandered into dangerous territory. The moral climate of our current status demands a change, and not simply a change that might come through an election cycle. The change needed is possible, but it will come only through spiritual awakening.

So, here is the deal: our churches have grown stale, and in many cases too silent on the salient issues of society. The prophet Micah asked, and answered, a question that cannot be ignored by the church, *"What does the Lord require of you but to do justice, and to love kindness, and to walk humbly with your God?"* Combine that with the fact that Jesus said this of the church, *"I will build my church and the gates of hell shall not prevail against it."*

Missing today is that image Jesus gave us of a militant church. Not a church on the defensive. Not a church seeking to blend in with a culture. Not a church unwilling to confront sin, and to call it sin. Modern Christianity has become the revised version of John Bunyan's "Pilgrim's Progress." Bunyan had his main character, Christian, distracted from his journey by Mr. Worldly Wiseman. Mr. Wiseman proposed that deliverance was available through Legality and Civility. That should sound familiar to our current status in America. Yes indeed, we need less lawlessness and more civility, but that will not be enough to save us. Jesus Christ alone can do that. To that end Jesus is still looking for a few disciples who will answer the call to, *"Come follow me,"* and *"Go tell."* What will your answer be?

ABOUT THE AUTHOR

Though a native of Alabama, Alan has lived in Chattanooga, Tennessee, for more than forty years. He grew up in the rural community of Elmore, near Wetumpka, Alabama. Following graduation from Wetumpka High School he moved to Birmingham, Alabama to begin his educational and career pursuits.

He is both an ordained minister and a Certified Financial Planner (CFP©). His ministry now spans more than fifty years, and he has more than thirty-five years of experience as a financial planner. He has served as Senior Pastor of churches in Alabama and Tennessee and was a founding partner of Oracle Wealth Management (a branch of Ameriprise Financial) in Chattanooga, Tennessee For the past 35 years Alan has also served as a Teaching Pastor for Abba's House (Central Baptist Church) in Chattanooga.

Alan is also the founder and leader of Path2truth Ministry. He continues to preach and teach and some of that ministry is available on the ministry website as well as Youtube. Paththth2truth has as its mission "to teach and preach the good news of Jesus Christ – in so doing, to bring Christians into a fresh encounter with God, to equip and encourage the church to be authentic, and to empower believers to share God's redemptive message."

Alan earned his BA degree from the University of Mobile and

additionally holds five advanced degrees and three professional certifications. Those degrees and certifications cover such disciplines as History, Theology, Counseling, Finance and Conflict Management. His educational pursuits spanned Samford University, the University of Mobile, Luther Rice Seminary, UT-Chattanooga, The American College and The University of Alabama.

Alan is an avid reader and writer, and is as well, an avid fan of college football and basketball. As time permits, he enjoys playing golf.

Most important of all…Alan is a husband to Dowdy, a father to Joy and Jennifer and "G"-daddy to grandchildren Ollie, Maggie, Alex and Benjamin.

Made in the USA
Middletown, DE
25 October 2022

13416209R00091